ASHE Higher Education Report: Volume 32, Number 3
Kelly Ward, Lisa E. Wolf-Wendel, Series Editors

Diversity Leadership in Higher Education

Adalberto Aguirre, Jr.
Rubén O. Martinez

Diversity Leadership in Higher Education
Adalberto Aguirre, Jr., Rubén O. Martinez
ASHE Higher Education Report: Volume 32, Number 3
Kelly Ward, Lisa Wolf-Wendel, Series Editors

ISSN 1551-6970   electronic ISSN 1554-6306   ISBN 0-7879-9578-9

The ASHE Higher Education Report is part of the Jossey-Bass Higher and Adult Education Series and is published six times a year by Wiley Subscription Services, Inc., A Wiley Company, at Jossey-Bass, 989 Market Street, San Francisco, California 94103-1741.

For subscription information, see the Back Issue/Subscription Order Form in the back of this volume.

CALL FOR PROPOSALS: Prospective authors are strongly encouraged to contact Kelly Ward (kaward@wsu.edu) or Lisa Wolf-Wendel (lwolf@ku.edu). See "About the ASHE Higher Education Report Series" in the back of this volume.

Visit the Jossey-Bass Web site at **www.josseybass.com.**

Printed in the United States of America on acid-free recycled paper.

Advisory Board

The ASHE Higher Education Report Series is sponsored by the Association for the Study of Higher Education (ASHE), which provides an editorial advisory board of ASHE members.

Contents

Executive Summary

Major shifts in population diversity have created significant pressures for all societal institutions, including higher education. As a social force, diversity promotes the importance of incorporating difference in building cohesive institutional arrangements that address structural barriers and organizational cultures that limit opportunities for members of ethnic and racial minority groups. Leadership is very important to diversity because it has the potential for developing and implementing practices in organizational culture that are inclusive of diversity. Diversity leadership, in particular, serves as a critical change agent for promoting initiatives that build inclusive social relations in higher education for integrating the multidimensional character of diversity with organizational culture.

This monograph examines and discusses the context for diversity leadership roles and practices in higher education by using research and theoretical and applied literatures from a variety of fields, including the social sciences, business, and higher education. Framing the discussion on leadership in this monograph is the perspective that American organizations tend to adapt to changes in their environment by seeking to co-opt features of that environment. Guided by the core value of efficiency, organizations seek to stay the course in a changing environment by employing co-optation approaches rather than transforming themselves to fit the new environment. It is the case with regard to institutions of higher education and their use of window-dressing approaches and token outcomes to disguise the marginalization of diversity in organizational culture. In short, colleges and universities seek to co-opt aspects of diversity to avoid changing their basic processes and practices.

The U.S. Supreme Court's decision in *Grutter* v. *Bollinger* reaffirmed the view that diversity is an important social force in higher education that poses important challenges for institutional arrangements that have not responded adequately to the increasing racial and ethnic diversity in the U.S. population. The argument made in this monograph is that institutions of higher education must develop leadership capacities to promote diversity as a positive social force and to portray diversity as a necessary institutional building block in the twenty-first century. In particular, the next phase in higher education leadership requires diversity leadership that is transformational for both higher education and society.

How Do the American Public and Primary Stakeholders in Higher Education Perceive Diversity Initiatives in Higher Education?

The American public and primary stakeholders in higher education (staff, students, and faculty) believe that the context for diversity in higher education must be enhanced. They believe it is necessary to increase the representation of racial and ethnic minority faculty and students and to change curricula to incorporate multicultural perspectives. The American public and primary stakeholders in higher education perceive a need for changing the context for diversity in higher education to better prepare students to live and work in an increasingly diverse society and workplace.

What Is the Nexus for Diversity and Leadership in the Organizational Culture of Higher Education?

A discussion of the nexus for diversity and leadership in higher education is hampered by conceptual and definitional issues in its organizational culture. Conceptually, diversity is treated as a social phenomenon associated with people located on the margins of society. As a result, diversity is defined as the structural position of racial and ethnic minority people in society, a structural position in society that marginalizes and excludes persons in society. The challenge then for institutions of higher education is to develop leadership roles and practices that integrate diversity as a valued social force and process in the organizational culture of higher education.

How Does Diversity Leadership Challenge the Organizational Culture in Higher Education?

On the surface, diversity leadership may not be compatible with the organizational culture in higher education. In general, it is assumed that a high index of homogeneity must be present among organizational members for leadership to find expression. In contrast, diversity is a social force that challenges homogeneity in the organizational culture. The challenge of diversity leadership to the organizational culture in higher education is to use the centrality of leadership to organizational integrity while incorporating diversity as an emergent dimension in organizational design.

How Do Institutions of Higher Education Use Organizational Practices to Respond to Diversity?

Institutions of higher education are challenged to develop organizational strategies that respond to diversity. Generally, institutions of higher education have used two types of organizational practices to frame their response to diversity issues: co-optation and transformation. They have used co-optation organizational strategies to treat diversity as a descriptive dimension in the organizational culture. That is, co-optation organizational strategies use diversity to create superficial images through such processes as window dressing and tokenism. In contrast, some institutions of higher education have begun to use transformational organizational strategies to treat diversity as a social force. That is, transformational organizational strategies promote diversity as an agent of change in the organizational culture.

What Is the Next Phase for Diversity Leadership in Higher Education?

The increasing racial and ethnic diversity in U.S. society will continue to challenge institutions of higher education to develop leadership roles and practices that are inclusive of diversity. The next phase for diversity leadership requires that institutions of higher education promote leadership practices that lead for diversity because they change organizational culture by reframing diversity as an inclusive process in a learning organization. The next phase for diversity leadership also requires that institutions of higher education remove from their organizational culture leadership practices that are selective in their response to diversity—practices that seek only to incorporate diversity as a descriptive and static organizational element rather than as a positive and dynamic social force.

Foreword

In an earlier ASHE monograph, Daryl Smith explained that diversity in higher education has four dimensions—access, climate, curriculum, and institutional transformation (Smith and Wolf-Wendel, *The Challenge of Diversity: Involvement or Alienation in the Academy?* Volume 31, Number 1, 2005)—dimensions that are separate but connected. Using this framework, Smith makes the case that institutions of higher education have not made sufficient progress in terms of any of these dimensions. Students, faculty, and administrations still are not as diverse as they might be, given the makeup of the larger U.S. population. Disparities in access are especially present at the more prestigious institutions and at the highest levels of leadership. Many campus constituents still perceive the campus climate at most colleges and universities as inhospitable or "chilly," and the climate does not seem to be improving particularly rapidly. Further, although progress has been made in diversifying the curriculum, the backlash against expanding what students ought to be exposed to is pervasive. It is the area of institutional transformation, however, where the least amount of progress has been made in terms of diversity. The leadership of most institutions of higher education still looks much like it did earlier and still operates under many of the same paradigms as before. It is difficult to find institutions that have really transformed themselves beyond an "add and stir" approach to diversity.

This monograph focuses on Smith's last dimension of diversity—institutional transformation. Aguirre and Martinez argue that institutions of higher education have merely given lip service to diversity and have treated diversity as window dressing rather than truly transforming the way they do business.

Getting complex institutions to change is undoubtedly a slow and frustrating process. Change never occurs as rapidly as one might like—and sometimes inertia is sufficient to maintain the status quo. In the face of inertia, Aguirre and Martinez argue that colleges and universities, and especially their leaders, need to go beyond adding new faces and need to approach diversity more holistically. To make institutional transformation possible requires leaders who think differently about diversity and how to lead.

The recent ASHE monograph by Kezar, Carducci, and Contreras-McGavin (*Rethinking the "L" Word in Higher Education: The Revolution of Research on Leadership,* Volume 31, Number 6, 2006) offers further insight into the issues raised in Aguirre and Martinez's monograph. Kezar and her colleagues argue that changes in higher education require leaders to have different skills and perspectives than in the past. To prepare today's leaders, they suggest changing the leadership paradigm to include thinking about leadership as a collective process involving teamwork and collaboration. Aguirre and Martinez make essentially a similar argument. In addition, they combine the extensive literature on diversity concerns with the literature on leadership to make the case that if institutions of higher education can embrace new leadership paradigms, perhaps they can make progress related to diversity. Until institutions can see beyond diversity as being a problem to solve rather than a means to improving quality, however, colleges and universities will remain as they are. Aguirre and Martinez offer us many insights on how to rethink both leadership and diversity to move them closer and to make them synonymous with institutional quality.

Lisa E. Wolf-Wendel
Series Editor

Acknowledgments

The ideas expressed in this monograph have been germinating for several years. We have benefited greatly from colleagues who have challenged us to develop a framework that identifies the centrality of diversity to higher education leadership. We were both very lucky to have been present during Tomas Rivera's tenure as chancellor of the University of California at Riverside in the late 1970s and early 1980s. He opened a window on leadership that revealed the need for challenging institutions of higher education to incorporate racial and ethnic minority people as full participants in the organizational culture of higher education. We also thank Adriana Kezar and Lisa Wolf-Wendel for supporting this monograph and encouraging us to pursue its completion. In addition, the anonymous reviewers were instrumental in bringing needed clarity and coherence to this monograph.

Published online in Wiley InterScience
(www.interscience.wiley.com) • DOI: 10.1002/aehe.3203

Diversity in Higher Education: Perceptions, Opinions, and Views

THE MERE MENTION OF THE WORD *DIVERSITY* in discussions of higher education often results in technical arguments about affirmative action and moral discussions about merit. In general, however, the word *diversity* refers to difference resulting from social changes in society. For example, the influx of immigrants from a large number of countries into the United States is a vehicle for introducing differences—linguistic, social, and cultural—into the U.S. population. As a social force in society, diversity has the potential to alter the complexion of a population and require change in societal institutions. At the same time, diversity is pregnant with turmoil when it challenges societal institutions to alter their structure.

Education is one of the most visible institutions in society, and its response to diversity has attracted considerable attention from the U.S. public. Given the importance placed in society on earning credentials from institutions of higher education, the topic of diversity in higher education is unsurprisingly a racing firestorm that responds to the ebb and flow of public opinion. For those interested in studying how institutions of higher education will respond to diversity in the twenty-first century, the U.S. Supreme Court's decisions in *Grutter* v. *Bollinger* (539 U.S. 244 [2003]) and Gratz v. *Bollinger* were viewed as important to slowing down but not stopping the firestorm in higher education. One purpose in this monograph is to give shape and size to the topic of diversity in higher education by focusing on one element of organizational structure and culture, leadership.

A caveat is in order regarding our use of the word *diversity* in this monograph. We treat it as a marker of population differences in society that are identifiable by status characteristics such as age, gender, race, sexual orientation, ethnicity, disability, and religion. As such, diversity refers to those characteristics that make individuals different from each other. As we discuss in this chapter, the nexus for discussions of diversity in higher education is rooted in Justice Powell's decision in *University of California* v. *Bakke* (438 U.S. 265 [1978]) regarding the role of diversity rationales using race as one factor for introducing heterogeneity into student populations in higher education. One result of Justice Powell's decision was that the attention generated by diversity rationales in higher education became focused on how institutions of higher education responded to changes in the racial and ethnic composition of U.S. society. Another result was that the word *diversity* became a marker of ethnic and racial representation in higher education. As Fullinwider (1997) noted, "When universities list their diversity policies, set up offices of diversity affairs, and measure their progress in achieving diversity, the word in every case is a synonym for minority/gender representation" (p. 1). To facilitate our discussion of diversity in higher education, we limit our use of the word *diversity* to discuss the participation of racial and ethnic minorities in leadership roles and positions in higher education.

To avoid confusion in this monograph, we separate *diversity* from its cousin *affirmative action.* Too often discussions about diversity initiatives in higher education are treated as discussions of equity, discussions that are more properly nested with the topic of affirmative action. For our purpose in this monograph, we treat diversity as a social force with a specific locus in population change in society. We treat affirmative action as a product of legal compromises that challenge higher education to respond to issues of equity. We recognize that a synergistic relationship exists between diversity and affirmative action in higher education, but we stop short of using them interchangeably in our discussion of diversity initiatives in higher education.

Purpose and Organization of the Monograph

This monograph examines and discusses the context for diversity leadership roles and practices in higher education by using research and theoretical and applied literatures from a variety of fields, including the social sciences, business, and higher education. Framing the discussion on leadership in this monograph is the perspective that American organizations respond to changes in their environment by seeking to co-opt features of that environment. Regarding diversity, the argument is advanced in this monograph that guided by the core value of efficiency, organizations respond to a changing environment by employing co-optive approaches rather than transforming themselves to fit the new environment. We argue in this monograph that co-optive versus transformational organizational responses result in different forms of leadership in higher education regarding diversity. We also argue in this monograph that institutions of higher education have responded to diversity by developing and promoting initiatives that seek only to window dress diversity or to create token opportunities for the expression of diversity.

To enhance our understanding of how institutions of higher education respond to diversity, especially initiatives that focus on leadership, each chapter in this monograph is designed to serve as a window for observing how diversity is shaped and promoted in different contexts in American higher education. The monograph is intended to serve as a primer on organizational theory regarding the association between leadership and diversity in higher education. The purpose of this chapter is to discuss public perceptions of diversity and its importance to higher education strategies and initiatives. It provides the reader with an overview of the issues and concerns that diversity leadership must address in higher education. The purpose of the next chapter is to discuss the organizational context for diversity in leadership roles and practices in higher education and the challenge posed by diversity leadership to traditional models of organizational culture in higher education. It provides the reader with the language and ideas necessary for a conceptual discussion of the challenges faced by diversity in the organizational culture and climate of higher education. "Diversity and Organizational Leadership in Higher Education" provides an overview of leadership models that underlie diversity strategies in higher education to develop a typology of diversity strategies that can serve as a heuristic tool for assessing the relative effectiveness of diversity strategies in relation to students, staff, faculty, and administrators. The chapter's purpose is to provide readers with a road map for navigating the organizational literature on diversity leadership strategies and practices. Finally, "Practicing

Diversity Leadership in Higher Education" uses the conceptual framework for diversity leadership strategies developed in the previous chapter to discuss the effects of diversity leadership on the organizational culture and institutional climate in higher education to build cultural competency among stakeholders in higher education. In particular, the final chapter advances the argument that proficient diversity leadership is important for building culturally proficient institutions of higher education.

Chapter One Tasks

To enhance our understanding of the issues and concerns surrounding diversity in higher education, this chapter discusses perceptions of diversity, the importance of diversity in higher education, and the outcomes of institutional diversity strategies. Our task in this chapter is to provide an overview of the persistent challenges faced by diversity initiatives in higher education. We start with Justice Powell's discussion of diversity rationales in higher education. We believe that this is an important starting point, because Justice Powell's decision in *Bakke* served as a catalyst for public debates and opinion about the responsibility institutions of higher education have in responding to racial and ethnic changes in the U.S. population. For our purpose in this chapter, a review of the diversity rationale in higher education is crucial for situating an examination of how the public perceives diversity initiatives in higher education. To this end, two questions serve as guides for the discussion in this chapter:

What is the public's perception of diversity initiatives in higher education?

How are diversity initiatives perceived by faculty, staff, and students in higher education?

The Diversity Rationale in Higher Education

The U.S. Supreme Court significantly shaped the context for diversity in higher education through its decision in *Bakke,* in which Alan Bakke, a white male, challenged the validity of a special admissions program at the University of California at Davis School of Medicine after having twice been denied admission. The medical school filled sixteen of its one hundred slots in its entering class through a special admissions program only open to minority applicants who were compared among themselves and not with the overall applicant pool. Bakke's college grade point average and MCAT score were among the highest among all the applicants and higher than all the minority applicants admitted to the medical school through the special admissions program. In *Bakke,* the U.S. Supreme Court affirmed the California Supreme Court's decision that the special admissions program had violated the equal protection clause of the Fourteenth Amendment, directed that the plaintiff be admitted to the School of Medicine, and reversed the judgment prohibiting the defendant from considering race in its future admissions.

Justice Lewis Powell, Jr., wrote in his opinion regarding *Bakke* that "ethnic diversity is only one element in a range of factors a university properly may consider in attaining the goal of a heterogeneous student body" (quoted in Parloff, 2002, p. 1). Powell wrote in the same opinion, however, that quotas "would hinder rather than further attainment of genuine diversity" (p. 1). Justice Powell's decision resulted in the notion that a diversity rationale could be used in higher education as long as it did not "refuse to compare applicants of different races or establish a strict quota on the basis of race" (Perea, Delgado, Harris, and Wildman, 2000, p. 732). As such, the Supreme Court outlawed racial quotas in higher education but condoned the use of race as a selective factor for promoting institutional diversity.

Since the notion of a diversity rationale was derived from Justice Powell's decision in *Bakke,* it has become the target of legal challenges that seek to define the need for diversity initiatives in higher education and their use in promoting racial and ethnic diversity on college campuses. In 1992, for example, Cheryl J. Hopwood and three other white plaintiffs filed suit against the University of Texas School of Law, alleging that they were denied admission as a result of procedures granting preferences to black and Mexican American applicants. The Fifth District Court paid deference to the Supreme Court precedent in *Bakke* and declined to declare the school's use of racial preferences in its admissions process unconstitutional [*Hopwood* v. *State of Texas,* 861 F. Supp. 551 (W. D. Tex. 1994)].

Instead, the Court applied strict scrutiny to the law school's admissions process and found that the use of racial preferences for the purpose of achieving a diverse student body served a compelling state interest under the

Fourteenth Amendment. The Court also found that the use of racial classifications for overcoming the present effects of past discrimination served a compelling government interest. The Court ultimately found, however, that the law school's use of separate admissions procedures for minorities and nonminorities prevented any meaningful comparative evaluation among applicants of different races and was not narrowly tailored to achieve those compelling interests. Consequently, the Court declared that the law school's 1992 admissions procedures violated the Fourteenth Amendment.

Similarly, five years later in 1997, the diversity rationale came under scrutiny in two Michigan cases. In *Gratz* v. *Bollinger,* Jennifer Gratz and Patrick Hamacher filed a class action suit on behalf of themselves and all others similarly situated against the University of Michigan, alleging that the university's College of Literature, Science, and the Arts had violated Title VI of the Civil Rights Act and the Equal Protection Clause of the Fourteenth Amendment by using race as a factor in admissions. The District Court ruled in favor of the plaintiffs and declared the admissions programs in existence from 1995 through 1998 unconstitutional on the basis that they were not narrowly tailored to meet the interest of diversity under the standard of strict scrutiny. The court also found, however, the admissions programs in existence in 1999 and 2000 to be constitutional, not only arguing that admissions programs that consider race for other than remedial purposes are permitted by the Fourteenth Amendment but also asserting that "diversity in higher education, by its very nature, is a permanent and ongoing interest" (*Gratz v. Bollinger,* 122 F. Supp. 2d 811, E.D. Mich. 2000, at 38, p. 137).

In the second case, Barbara Grutter filed suit against the University of Michigan Law School after being denied admission. Grutter alleged that she was discriminated against on the basis of her race (Caucasian, "a disfavored racial group") and that the law school violated the Fourteenth Amendment and Title VI of the Civil Rights Act of 1964, which prohibits recipients of federal funds from discriminating on the basis of race (*Grutter* v. *Bollinger,* F. Supp. 2d 821, U. S. Dist. 2001, p. 137). In *Grutter,* the District Court found in favor of the plaintiff and against the law school. The court declared that the law school's use of race in its admissions decisions violated the Equal Protection Clause of the Fourteenth Amendment and Title VI of the Civil Rights

Act of 1964; it further prohibited the law school from using race as a factor in its admissions decisions. In turning to the constitutionality of using race as a factor in achieving racial diversity, the court disagreed with Justice Powell's opinion in *Bakke,* stating that "*Bakke* does not stand for the proposition that a university's desire to assemble a racially diverse student body is a compelling state interest" (p. 77). The court went on to suggest that diversity could have an important educational benefit but made a distinction between diversity of viewpoint and racial diversity and declared, "the connection between race and viewpoint is tenuous, at best" (p. 83).

On May 14, 2002, a sharply divided Sixth Circuit Court of Appeals voted five to four to overturn the lower court's ruling that the admissions policy used by the University of Michigan Law School illegally discriminated against white applicants (Fletcher, 2002; Steinberg, 2002). The court distinguished between remedial and nonremedial considerations of race and ethnicity and determined that the requirement of a "definite stopping point" applied to the first and not the second consideration. The majority opinion for the court noted that the law school's admissions policy set appropriate limits on the competitive consideration of race and ethnicity. The court also noted in its opinion that the law school intended to consider race and ethnicity to achieve a diverse and robust student body only until it became possible to enroll a "critical mass" of underrepresented minority students through race-neutral means. In contrast, the minority opinion (led by Judge Danny J. Boggs) noted that *Grutter* was a clear instance of racial discrimination by a state institution and that the law school did not seek diversity for education's sake, that diversity was simply a vehicle for increasing "racial number."

In *Grutter* v. *Bollinger,* the U.S. Supreme Court found that the U.S. Constitution did not prohibit the University of Michigan Law School from narrowly tailoring the use of race in admissions decisions to obtain the educational benefits from having a diverse student body. In writing the majority opinion for the Court, Justice Sandra Day O'Connor wrote: "It has been 25 years since Justice Powell first approved the use of race to further an interest in student body diversity in the context of public higher education. Since that time, the number of minority applicants with high grades and test scores has indeed increased. We expect that 25 years from now, the use of racial preferences will no longer be necessary to further the interest approved today" (p. 31).

Justice O'Connor's observation that in twenty-five years the use of racial preferences would no longer be necessary for promoting student diversity has implications for organizational leadership in higher education. From a general perspective, her observation implies that organizational leadership in higher education will undergo a transformation in the next twenty-five years that will no longer require the use of institutional initiatives that specifically target diversity. It appears then that Justice O'Connor has provided a twenty-five-year window of opportunity for incorporating diversity into organizational leadership in higher education.

What can one observe from the preceding discussion regarding the context for diversity in higher education? It is certainly clear that diversity has been a major concern for institutions of higher education for more than a quarter century. *Bakke* was the catalyst for a public discourse regarding the use of a "diversity rationale" for changing the racial and ethnic composition of student populations in higher education. *Hopwood* reinforced the use of a "diversity rationale" but only if it did not result in race-specific admission processes in higher education. Similarly, *Gratz* affirmed the pursuit of diversity in higher education as an ongoing interest in higher education, and *Grutter* supported the use of race to achieve diversity in higher education. Diversity then is a social concern and a compelling legal interest for institutions of higher education.

Public Perceptions of Diversity Initiatives in Higher Education

As part of its campus diversity initiative, the Ford Foundation commissioned a survey of 2,011 registered voters in 1998. The initiative was created to communicate the value of diversity in higher education. In general, the survey's results found widespread support for college and university efforts to diversify the student body and to offer classes about different cultures (Lurie, 1998). The majority of survey respondents did not support the argument that diversity weakens the college environment. Rather, the majority of survey respondents

EXHIBIT 1
Public Opinion Regarding the Effects of Diversity Initiatives in Higher Education

Question: Overall, would you say that efforts to have a more diverse student body on college campuses have a more positive or negative effect on the education of students?
Responses: Very Positive (31%)   Somewhat Positive (44%)   Negative (18%) NA (7%)

Question: Overall, would you say diversity on campus has a more positive or negative effect on the general atmosphere on campus?
Responses: Very Positive (22%)   Somewhat Positive (47%)   Negative (22%) NA (9%)

Question: Overall, would you say that courses and campus activities emphasizing diversity have a more positive or negative effect on the education of college students?
Responses: Very Positive (24%)   Somewhat Positive (45%)   Negative (22%) NA (9%)

Note: Data derived from Ford Foundation campus diversity initiative, a national survey of 2,011 registered voters conducted July 14 to August 4, 1998.

stated that a diverse student body on college campuses has a positive effect on the education of students, diversity has a positive effect on a college's general atmosphere, and college activities and courses that emphasize diversity have a positive effect on the education of college students (see Exhibit 1).

Although the majority of survey respondents supported diversity initiatives in higher education, survey respondents stated that diversity is a significant challenge for higher education. For example, survey respondents were almost evenly split in their perception that diversity education should emphasize common American values (47 percent) or that diversity education should teach other people's cultures (45 percent). Although the majority of survey respondents (91 percent) perceived diversity education as necessary for living in a multicultural society, some survey respondents (48 percent) perceived diversity education as a source of conflict and division. Some survey respondents (38 percent) viewed diversity education as a means for admitting and graduating unqualified students in higher education.

Regarding perceptions of the problems diversity education poses in higher education, 37 percent of survey respondents perceived diversity education such as women's studies and Chicano studies as taking valuable resources from the education and training of students in general. Slightly more than one-third (34 percent) of survey respondents perceived diversity education as nothing more than political correctness. One-third (33 percent) of survey respondents perceived diversity education as making the college curriculum less rigorous. As such, although the overall context for diversity in higher education is favorable, one can identify problematic issues associated with the practice of diversity education in higher education.

Institutional Responsibility for Diversity

According to the Ford Foundation's campus diversity initiative survey, the American public believes that colleges and universities have a responsibility to promote diversity initiatives in American society (see Exhibit 2). The

EXHIBIT 2
Public Opinion Regarding Higher Education's Responsibility for Diversity Initiatives

1. Preparing people to function in a more diverse society.

Important	93%
Not Important	6%

2. Preparing people to function in a more diverse workforce.

Important	94%
Not Important	4%

3. Every student should study different cultures as a requisite for graduation.

Important	55%
Not Important	43%

4. College is not doing its job if graduates cannot get along in a diverse population.

Important	65%
Not Important	32%

Note: Data derived from Ford Foundation campus diversity initiative, a national survey of 2,011 registered voters conducted July 14 to August 4, 1998.

American public believes that it is important that colleges and universities prepare people to function in a more diverse society and in a more diverse workforce. Although the American public believes that every college student should study different cultures to graduate, a sizable sector (43 percent) of the American public does not believe it is necessary for graduation. Almost two-thirds of the American public believes that colleges and universities are not doing their job if graduates cannot get along in a diverse population.

The majority of the American public (52 percent) believes that introducing diversity concerns into college courses raises academic standards (see Exhibit 3). Only a small sector (15 percent) of the American public believes that introducing diversity initiatives into college courses lowers academic standards. The majority (85 percent) of the American public believes that faculty should incorporate information about diversity in American society into their courses. In addition, the majority of the American public (59 percent) does not believe that adding material about women and minorities to the college curriculum makes it less rigorous.

EXHIBIT 3
Public Opinion Regarding Diversity Initiatives in Higher Education

1. Course diversity . . .

Raises academic standards	52%
Lowers academic standards	15%
Neither	25%

2. Faculty should incorporate information about diversity in American society in their courses.

Agree	85%
Disagree	11%

3. Adding material about women and minorities to the college curriculum makes it less rigorous.

Agree	33%
Disagree	59%

Note: Data derived from Ford Foundation campus diversity initiative, a national survey of 2,011 registered voters conducted July 14 to August 4, 1998.

Purpose of Higher Education

Survey respondents perceived the purpose of higher education as providing students with basic skills (85 percent) and career training (72 percent). Two-thirds of survey respondents perceived the purpose of higher education as preparing people to function in a more diverse society and in a more diverse workplace. Slightly more than half the survey respondents (56 percent) perceived the purpose of higher education as preparing people for effective civic participation and leadership.

Perceptions of Diversity

Despite overwhelmingly supporting diversity in higher education, survey respondents had different interpretations of the word *diversity.* Fifty percent of survey respondents interpreted "diversity" as meaning different ethnicity, race, nationality, or culture. Some survey respondents (18 percent) interpreted "diversity" as referring to people with different thoughts and ideas. Some survey respondents (12 percent) interpreted "diversity" as referring to different social status or economic and education levels. Eight percent of survey respondents interpreted "diversity" to mean different religious backgrounds.

Despite having different interpretations of the word *diversity* 97 percent of survey respondents agreed that in the future people will need to get along with people who are not like them, 94 percent agreed that increasing diversity in the U.S. population makes it important that people understand people different from themselves, and 91 percent agreed that increasing globalization requires that people understand people who are different from themselves. A majority of survey respondents (58 percent) did not believe that diversity is being addressed effectively in American society.

Although Americans may perceive diversity as a social force in American society, especially one that challenges higher education to develop appropriate responses to diversity, Americans are unsure about higher education's response to diversity. Americans may believe that diversity is not being addressed effectively in American society, but how do they respond to initiatives designed to address concerns about diversity in higher education? Before the U.S. Supreme Court's review of *Grutter* and *Gratz,* the Quinnipiac University Polling Institute conducted a telephone survey of 1,448 persons between February 26 and March 3,

2003. People were asked to respond to the proposition that "race" could be used as a factor in college admissions to diversify the student body. Sixty-seven percent of survey respondents opposed the use of race in college admissions.

Similarly, the Gallup Organization conducted a telephone survey of 1,385 persons between June 12 and June 18, 2003. The survey asked people to evaluate their views on whether "merit" or "race/ethnicity" should be used as a selection factor in college admissions. The majority of survey respondents (69 percent) viewed merit as the primary factor in college admissions, even if it resulted in admitting fewer minority students. In contrast, 27 percent of survey respondents viewed race/ethnicity as necessary factors in college admissions to promote diversity on campus.

Americans see diversity as an aspect of American society that needs to be addressed, but they are reluctant to support initiatives that seek to diversify institutions of higher education. Americans do not support introducing race and ethnicity into the college admissions process as an adequate response. How do stakeholders in higher education—faculty, students, and administrators—perceive diversity initiatives in higher education? How do their views contrast with those of the American public?

Faculty, Student, and Administrator Perceptions of Diversity

Although the public perceives the need for diversity initiatives in higher education, how do faculty and students perceive diversity initiatives in higher education? A survey of University of Oregon students in 2002, for example, found that students did not believe the university was interested in diversity. According to the survey's results, 57 percent of students did not believe that the campus leadership fostered diversity, and 47 percent did not think the curriculum represented contributions from minority groups (Center on Diversity and Community, 2002). Similarly, in a poll of college students conducted in 2002, 84 percent of the students believed that ethnic diversity was important on campus; however, 77 percent of the students were opposed to giving preferences to minority students in the admissions process (Thernstrom, 2000).

In a 1999 cross-national study of 140 U.S. colleges and universities regarding attitudes toward diversity in higher education, Rothman, Lipset, and Nevitte (2002) found "widespread support for offering multicultural courses on American campuses, but not for requiring them" (p. 57). Selected results from the survey are presented in Table 1. Forty-five percent of the students felt that classes about the experiences of minorities should be made available on campus. In addition, slightly more than one-third (38 percent) of the students felt that classes about the experiences of minorities should be encouraged as part of the curriculum. Only 16 percent of the students believed that the classes should be required, however.

The majority of students (82 percent) did not agree with the statement that too much attention was paid to minority issues on campus. The majority (79 percent) felt that minority students were treated the same as white students on their own campus. Seventy-three percent of the students disagreed with the statement that minority group undergraduates should be admitted even if it meant relaxing standards. Finally, the majority (53 percent) of students felt that special admissions policies for minority students did not have any real impact on academic standards. The majority of students (65 percent) disagreed with the statement "Traditional standards of merit for jobs and school admission are basically affirmative action for white males." The majority of students (85 percent) agreed with the statement "No one should be given special preference in jobs or college admissions on the basis of their gender or race."

Umbach and Kuh (2003) examined data from the spring 2002 National Survey of Student Engagement (NSSE). The NSSE is an annual survey of first-year and senior college students that measures the participation of college students in educational practices linked to valued college outcomes. In general, Umbach and Kuh found that students at liberal arts colleges were significantly more likely than students at other types of institutions to engage in diversity-related activities and to report greater empathy for people from diverse backgrounds. Regarding the diversity experiences available to students at liberal arts colleges, Umbach and Kuh found that students who participated in diversity-related experiences reported "higher levels of academic challenge, greater opportunities for active and collaborative learning, and a more supportive campus environment" (p. 17).

TABLE 1
Opinion of Faculty, Students, and Administrators Regarding Campus Diversity Initiatives

Item	Faculty n = 1,594	Students n = 1,569	Administrators n = 789
Course diversity on campus			
Required	17%	16%	17%
Encouraged	42%	38%	46%
Made Available	40%	45%	35%
Too much attention is paid to minority issues			
Agree	12%	18%	7%
Disagree	87%	82%	93%
Minority faculty on campus are treated . . .			
Same as white faculty	72%	—	79%
Better than white faculty	12%	—	6%
Worse than white faculty	12%	—	14%
Minority students on campus are treated . . .			
Same as white students	73%	79%	76%
Better than white students	7%	6%	6%
Worse than white students	18%	14%	17%
"Traditional standards of merit for jobs and school admission are basically affirmative action for white males."			
Agree	31%	34%	24%
Disagree	67%	65%	72%
Relax admission standards for minority undergraduates			
Agree	41%	25%	43%
Disagree	57%	75%	55%
Relax academic requirements for hiring minority faculty			
Agree	18%	24%	17%
Disagree	81%	76%	82%
Impact of special admissions programs for minority students on academic standards			
Higher	3%	10%	2%
No real impact	57%	53%	66%
Lower	38%	35%	29%
Impact of special hiring policies for minority faculty on academic standards			
Higher	6%	13%	4%
No real impact	55%	58%	69%
Lower	36%	28%	24%

Source: Rothman, Lipset, and Nevitte (2002).

Faculty Perceptions

According to Rothman, Lipset, and Nevitte (2002), faculty at U.S. colleges and universities support campus diversity initiatives. Faculty are most likely to support the availability (40 percent) or encourage the availability (42 percent) of courses regarding the experience of racial minorities. Only a small percentage of faculty (17 percent) would require that courses on the experience of racial minorities be taught. The majority of faculty (87 percent) do not believe that their campus pays too much attention to minority issues. The majority of faculty believe that minority faculty are treated the same as white faculty and that minority students are treated the same as white students on their campus, 72 percent and 73 percent, respectively. Interestingly, in response to a question regarding which group faces the greatest difficulty getting hired for a faculty position at the average university (not shown on the table), 43 percent of the faculty felt that white males have a tougher time getting hired than minority females (19 percent), minority males (15 percent), or white females (10 percent).

The majority of faculty (67 percent) disagreed with the statement "Traditional standards of merit for jobs and school admission are basically affirmative action for white males." The majority of faculty (56 percent) also disagreed with the statement "No one should be given special preference in jobs or college admissions on the basis of . . . gender or race" (not shown on the table). Accordingly, the majority of faculty do not believe that admission standards should be relaxed for minority group undergraduates or that academic requirements should be relaxed for appointing minority group members to the faculty, 57 percent and 81 percent, respectively. Interestingly, the majority of faculty believe that special admissions policies for minority students and special hiring policies for minority faculty have no real impact on academic standards, 57 percent and 55 percent, respectively.

Administrators' Perceptions

A distinctive feature of the survey data reported by Rothman, Lipset, and Nevitte (2002) is the inclusion of administrators in colleges and universities. According to survey results, administrators are likely to encourage (42 percent) or support the availability of (39 percent) courses on the experiences of racial minorities. Only 17 percent of administrators would require that the courses be taught on their campus. The majority of administrators (93 percent) disagreed with the statement "This university pays too much attention to minority issues." The majority of administrators believe that minority faculty are treated the same as white faculty and that minority students are treated the same as white students on their campus, 77 percent and 76 percent, respectively. Regarding the hiring of faculty, administrators felt that white males (37 percent) would have a tougher time getting hired than minority males (18 percent), minority females (17 percent), and white females (12 percent).

The majority of administrators (72 percent) disagreed with the statement "Traditional standards of merit for jobs and school admission are basically affirmative action for white males." The majority of administrators do not believe that admission standards should be relaxed for minority group undergraduates or that academic requirements should be relaxed for hiring minority faculty, 55 percent and 82 percent, respectively. The majority of administrators believe, however, that special admissions policies for minority students and special hiring policies for minority faculty have no real impact on academic standards, 66 percent and 69 percent, respectively.

Competing Perceptions of Campus Diversity

The data in Table 1 allow for a comparison of faculty, students', and administrators' perceptions of diversity initiatives in higher education. According to the table, faculty, students, and administrators differ in their perceptions of diversity initiatives in several ways:

Regarding the issue of diversity in the curriculum (courses), faculty, students, and administrators are just as likely to require it on their campus; administrators are more likely to encourage course diversity but are less likely to support the availability of course diversity on their campus.

Students are more likely than faculty and administrators to agree that too much attention is paid to minority issues on their campus, while administrators are more likely to disagree.

Faculty are more likely than administrators to agree that minority faculty are treated better than white faculty on their campus; however, administrators are more likely to believe that minority faculty are treated the same as white faculty or worse than white faculty.

Faculty, students, and administrators are almost as likely to agree that minority students on their campus are treated the same as white students or better than white students; however, faculty and administrators are more likely than students to believe that minority students are treated worse than white students.

Faculty and students are almost as likely to agree with the statement "Traditional standards of merit for jobs and school admission are basically affirmative action for white males," while administrators are more likely to disagree with the statement.

Students are less likely than both faculty and administrators to agree that admission standards should be relaxed for minority undergraduates.

Faculty and administrators are more likely than students to disagree with relaxing academic requirements for hiring minority faculty.

Faculty, students, and administrators believe that special admissions programs for minority students have no real impact on academic standards; however, students are more likely to believe that they raise academic standards, and faculty are more likely to believe that they lower academic standards.

Faculty, students, and administrators believe that special hiring policies for minority faculty have no real impact on academic standards; however, students are more likely to believe that they raise academic standards, and faculty are more likely to believe that they lower academic standards.

Summary

Institutions of higher education are bellwethers of societal changes such as demographic factors that require attention regarding their inclusion. Institutions of higher education must develop and promote responses to diversity that communicate to society their recognition of changes taking place in society. The organizational culture in higher education, however, often resists change because it perceives it as a threat to existing values and beliefs (see Keup, Walker, Astin, and Lindholm, 2001). As a result, developing responses to diversity is a challenging task for institutions of higher education because they are perceived in society as custodians of knowledge—valued knowledge that affects the quality of life and well-being of society (Wilcox and Ebbs, 1992). In particular, diversity poses challenges for institutions of higher education with regard to their ability to transform the knowledge production process into one that promotes diversity as essential to improving society's well-being. That is, institutions of higher education must develop strategies for responding to diversity that communicate to society their ability to respond to societal change and their commitment to long-term change for the betterment of society. In this context then and given our review in this chapter of public and higher education stakeholders' perceptions of diversity in higher education, what responses or strategies do the public and stakeholders perceive as appropriate issues for higher education's response to diversity? This question serves as a synthesis of the two questions we set out to answer in this chapter:

What is the public's perception of diversity initiatives in higher education?

How are diversity initiatives perceived by faculty, staff, and students in higher education?

It is clear from our discussion and review of opinion data regarding diversity and U.S. institutions of higher education in this chapter that diversity in higher education is a concern shared by the American public and the stakeholders (faculty, students, and administrators) in higher education. First, the American public and stakeholders in higher education believe that a need exists for enhancing the context for diversity in higher education by increasing the representation of minority students and faculty. They recognize that diversity is linked to demographic changes taking place in society, especially the growing numbers of racial and ethnic minority persons in American society. In general, the context for diversity in higher education needs change, change that results in better-prepared students ready to live and work in an increasingly diverse society and workplace. In short, the public and stakeholders perceive institutions of higher education as responsible for providing students with the valued knowledge required for meeting the challenges of living in a diverse society.

Second, the American public and stakeholders perceive diversity initiatives such as the introduction of diversity issues or topics in the curriculum as positive contributions to the learning experiences of college students. Interestingly, both the public and stakeholders perceive the introduction of diversity into the college course curriculum as a contribution rather than a liability to academic standards. In particular, survey responses to the Ford Foundation's campus diversity initiative show that the American public supports various types of diversity initiatives in the college curriculum such as community-based internships and a team approach to teaching college courses. Does this support suggest that the public and stakeholders would promote changes in the curriculum that might result in a much more multicultural culture in higher education?

Third, the American public and stakeholders do not perceive diversity initiatives as a threat to academic culture. Diversity is not perceived as contributing to conflict or division, as a drain on valuable institutional resources, as a mechanism for admitting unqualified students, or as a response to political correctness. As a result, one can observe that the American public and stakeholders do not perceive diversity initiatives in higher education as contributing to the breakdown of academic culture or as diverting valuable resources from a college's mission to educate students. It would appear then that the public and stakeholders do not perceive diversity as an obstacle to higher education's role as a custodian of knowledge in society. Can one interpret it to mean that the public and stakeholders perceive institutional responses to diversity as part of higher education's ability to transform itself as it responds to societal changes?

Fourth, the American public and stakeholders in higher education do not support diversity initiatives that would relax academic requirements for admitting minority students or for the hiring of minority faculty. Although the American public and stakeholders identify the need to address diversity concerns in higher education, they do not support relaxing academic requirements for minority students and faculty. Can one say that the public and stakeholders perceive limitations to higher education's ability to transform itself in its response to societal changes? It is clear that the public and stakeholders do not support relaxing certain elements of the culture in higher education. One might observe that the public and stakeholders may perceive diversity as an important concern for higher education but not important enough to promote altering practices that determine entry into institutions of higher education.

Finally, given our review and discussion of opinion data, one is led to wonder whether the American public and stakeholders perceive relaxing academic requirements as "affirmative action" that benefits only a few persons. If so, then our review of public opinion suggests that the American public and stakeholders in higher education distinguish between institutional initiatives that benefit a few persons (affirmative action) and institutional initiatives that infuse diverse experiences (diversity) into the academic culture. If this observation is valid, then it supports our contention that "diversity" and "affirmative action" must be treated as two separate yet synergistically tied concepts. The distinction is even more important for decision makers in higher education who make strategic responses that address the needs of society without endangering the promotion of issues in the academic culture (such as diversity) that might be perceived as benefiting only a few persons or groups in society.

Diversity, Leadership, and Organizational Culture in Higher Education

JUSTICE POWELL'S DISCUSSION OF THE DIVERSITY RATIONALE in *Bakke* may have been a recognition of the emerging significance of diversity as a social force destined to alter institutional environments in the United States, especially in higher education. By focusing on the use of the diversity rationale to alter the organizational culture in higher education, Justice Powell's decision serves as a starting point for considering the institutional environment for diversity leadership in higher education.

Public and stakeholder opinions of diversity in higher education, for example, can instruct us regarding aspects of the organizational culture in higher education that are linked with the development and support of diversity initiatives in higher education. Based on the opinion data reviewed in the previous chapter, the U.S. public and stakeholders in higher education perceive a need for colleges and universities to address the issues and concerns raised by diversity initiatives. Although public and stakeholder opinions identify curriculum changes as an important aspect of the organizational culture that can be altered, their opinions generally do not support the creation of special admissions programs for minority students or the creation of special recruitment programs for minority faculty. As a result, some aspects of the organizational culture in higher education receive public support for change and some do not to accommodate initiatives that target diversity.

This chapter discusses issues and concerns regarding the organizational culture for leadership that focuses on diversity issues and concerns in U.S. higher education. Our primary concern in this chapter is with predominantly white institutions of higher education. Two questions serve as guides for discussion in this chapter:

What is the organizational culture for leadership roles and practices that address diversity issues and concerns in higher education?

What challenges do leadership roles and practices that address diversity issues and concerns pose for the organizational culture in higher education?

In the previous chapter, we used public and stakeholder opinions of diversity initiatives in higher education to identify and discuss aspects of the institutional environment that would support diversity initiatives. As such, the institutional environment is perceived as capable of responding to diversity concerns either by supporting or resisting pressures for change. This chapter examines how the organizational culture in higher education accommodates or responds to leadership roles or practices focused on diversity. More important, an examination of the importance of leadership that addresses diversity issues and concerns in the organizational culture of higher education enhances our understanding of the synergistic association between diversity and leadership in higher education. To this end, this chapter explores why the study of organizational culture in higher education is important to discussions of diversity and leadership.

This chapter focuses on organizational culture, leadership, and diversity. Our notion of organizational culture is similar to Pettigrew's definition (1979) of organizational culture as the "amalgam of beliefs, ideology, language, ritual, and myth" (p. 572). Similarly, Masland (2000) refers to organizational culture as the "implicit values, beliefs, and ideologies of those within an organization" (p. 147). To these views of organizational culture we add the day-to-day practices of organizations—practices that embody the values of the different groups making up particular organizations. We also consider organizational culture as the glue that holds an organization together. Regarding higher education, Clark (1972) refers to the academic culture as an organizational saga that is a "collective understanding of unique accomplishment in a formally established group" (p. 179). According to Clark, the organizational saga serves to strengthen the association of students, staff, and faculty with the values and beliefs of higher education.

We treat leadership as a dynamic aspect of organizational culture that can transform higher education into a responsive and adaptive organization (see Selznick, 1957). Leadership in higher education is often treated as transformational, that is, capable of promoting change in the organization and in the organization's relationship with its environment. For example, Astin and Astin (2000) offer a working definition for transformational leadership in higher education by outlining possible outcomes: "to enable and encourage faculty, students, administrators, and other staff to change and transform institutions so that they can more effectively enhance student learning and development, generate knowledge, and serve the community, and . . . to empower students to become agents of positive social change in the larger society" (p. 9). As such, and for our purpose in this monograph, transformational leadership seeks to change values and preferences that promote an exclusionary organizational culture in higher education for diverse populations (Aguirre and Martinez, 2002).

In general, diversity is a concept used to recognize difference. Diversity recognizes that everyone is different and that different backgrounds should be respected. People exhibit status characteristics such as race, ethnicity, gender, and religion that identify them as different. As such, diversity promotes a positive attitude toward difference. The *Diversity Dictionary* defines diversity as "a situation that includes representation of multiple (ideally all) groups within a prescribed environment, such as a university or a workplace. This word most commonly refers to differences between cultural groups, although it is also used to describe differences within cultural groups, [for example,] diversity within the Asian-American culture [that] includes Korean Americans and Japanese Americans. An emphasis on accepting and respecting cultural differences by recognizing that no one culture is intrinsically superior to another underlies the current usage of the term" (www.inform.umd.edu/EdRes/Topic/Diversity/Reference/divdic.htm). We treat diversity as a marker of differences between cultural groups. Specifically, we use the word *diversity* in relationship to racial and ethnic minority groups and how institutions of higher education have developed leadership initiatives that respond to diversity issues and concerns.

This chapter uses the research literature to develop a framework for discussing the links between organizational culture, diversity, and leadership. Given the task we have set for ourselves in this chapter, the framework we develop instructs one regarding the organizational responses that diversity requires in higher education. In doing so, we subscribe to DiTomaso and Hooijberg's observations (1996) that studies of diversity leadership have "been mostly about developing awareness of differences rather then about leadership skills from the perspective of diversity" (p. 164). To this end, we start our discussion in this chapter by examining how competing perspectives introduced by the discourse on learning and postmodern organizations have transformed the discourse on leadership in higher education organizations. We then proceed with a review of the research literature to discuss the constitutive features of leadership in higher education. We follow this discussion by examining how shifts have occurred in the organizational culture of higher education as it responds to diversity. From there we proceed to a discussion of how diversity leadership, as an outcome of the interface between diversity and leadership, is positioned in the organizational culture of higher education.

Changing Organizational Culture

The transition from the twentieth to the twenty-first century has been a period of great social structural turbulence and increased societal complexity, attended by new organizational forms and an intensification of intergroup relations (Amaral and Magalhā, 2003; Arthur and Shapiro, 1995). The transition period gave rise to new theories of society, organizations, and leadership, including the rise of the postmodern paradigm, which turned the basic principles of modernism and knowledge production on their heads. The postmodern paradigm promoted the perspective that the organization is a collective projection of organizational members, with leaders serving as visionaries that inspire change (Keough and Tobin, 2001; Weinstein and Weinstein, 1998). The most prominent emphasis in leadership theory has been the prescription to transform organizations to better align them with the dynamics of an emergent economic (and political) global order (Golembiewski and Kuhnert, 1994; Vicere, 1995).

As a result of social and economic structural shifts focused on making the relationship between worker and organization more efficient, major institutions in society have sought to transfer knowledge from workers to management as a means of improving organizational operations. According to Gephart (1996), management theory promoted the idea that in transferring knowledge from workers to managers, "management education was developed in an effort to create a force or 'carrier' for technical rationality in organizations" (p. 92). At the same time, changes in the racial and ethnic demographic character of the U.S. population prompted scholars such as Thomas and Ely (1996) to exhort organizations to embrace diversity beyond the simple levels of passive representation and minimal compliance with federal and state laws to one including ethnic and racial minorities in meaningful ways in organizational learning. These groups ". . . bring different, important, and competitively relevant knowledge and perspectives about how to actually *do work*—how to design processes, reach goals, frame tasks, create effective teams, communicate ideas, and lead" (p. 80). Consequently, organizations must adapt not only to structural changes in society to become more competitive but also to increasing racial and ethnic diversity in society.

The first major transfer of production knowledge from workers to management occurred at the turn of the twentieth century when Frederick Taylor and other proponents of scientific management improved industrial organizations by transferring knowledge of production techniques from workers to managers (Gabor, 2000). The transfer occurred by enlisting the participation of workers in the design of the "one best way" to complete production tasks (Jaffee, 2001). One hundred years later, at the close of the twentieth century, workers were once again enlisted in designing and redesigning organizations and their operational processes. This time it was under the framework of "learning organizations," a perspective developed by leadership gurus such as Argyris and Schön (1978, 1996) and popularized by Senge (1990) and a multitude of scholarly writers (see, for example, Easterby-Smith, Araujo, and Burgoyne, 1999; Freed and Klugman, 1996). The term *learning organization* was applied to those organizations in which members are constantly learning, especially ideal educational organizations (see, for example, Coppieters, 2005; Giles and Hargreaves, 2006).

In higher education, application of the ideas and concepts associated with a learning organization has had limited appeal to faculty, perhaps because they perceive the learning organization as a form of Taylorism rooted in total quality management (TQM) techniques (English, 1997). The ideas and concepts associated with the learning organization under the rubric of TQM, however, have appealed to policymakers and administrators in higher education because they offer the ability to "manage" and "process" accountability of how the university works as an organization (Bensimon, 1995). According to Kezar (2005), the confusion regarding the application in higher education of ideas and concepts associated with the learning organization has resulted in a perception that "people on campus are concerned that the learning organization is a management fad" (p. 7). Similarly, Birnbaum (2000b) notes that the idea of a learning organization is confusing when it is applied to higher education institutions: "The failure of planning programming budgeting systems, management by objectives, and zero based budgeting everywhere it was tried might have served as a cautionary tale. It could have reminded us how complicated universities are, how little we know about how they work, and how well intentioned, but misguided attempts to rationalize their affairs could lead to confusion rather than improved effectiveness" (p. 63).

The framework of a learning organization, with its emphasis on motivating the organization to act collectively, emphasizes the application of transformational leadership as necessary for enhancing the capacity of organizations to reinvent themselves to meet the exigencies of the global economy. The conceptual work by Argyris and Schön (1978) in the 1970s on double-loop learning in organizations and later on learning organizations was translated into prescriptive theories combining learning and systems models for organizational survival strategies in contexts of rapidly changing environmental conditions (Coopey, 1995). As a result, the purpose of transformational leadership is not so much to change individuals as it is to transform organizational culture (roles and practices) to meet the demands from a changing social environment (for an example of transformational leadership in education, see Hartley, 2004). As such, the purpose of transformational leadership is to develop an organization's ability to adapt, to search for adaptive strategies.

The focus on transformational leadership in the learning organization severely tested the use of diversity to promote organizational change, given the limited social and human capital investment in diversity by learning organizations (Aguirre, forthcoming). Unsurprisingly, the learning organization was challenged by postmodern perspectives that stressed the need for higher education organizations to respond to three changes taking place in society: revolutionary technological advances, emphasis on diversity, and the acceptance of innovation and change (Beck, 1993; Bergquist, 1993). From a postmodern perspective, diversity is seen not only as a factor in the expansion of knowledge but also as necessary for linking personal growth to organizational change. In particular, diversity challenges higher education to incorporate heterogeneous strategies into its organizational culture to make sense of leadership roles and practices that target diversity (see Ayers, 2005; Thorne-Beckerman, 1999). In addition, from a postmodern perspective "new" organizational space must be conceived to actualize diversity in higher education's organizational culture (Bergquist, 1998; Ford and Harding, 2004). Organizational roles and practices focused on diversity are thus nested in the "new" organizational space. In a sense, this new organizational space is similar to Burt's notion (1992, 2000) of "structural holes theory": roles and practices focused on diversity reside in parts of the organizational culture that are undervalued or seen as having limited social capital. The aim of leadership roles and practices focused on diversity is to transform higher education's organizational culture to incorporate diversity with the values and practices of higher education.

In summary, the discourse on theory and leadership practices in higher education has been affected by the concepts and leadership frameworks that emerged from a postmodernist perspective on learning organizations (for example, Birnbaum, 2000a; Bloland, 1995; English, 1998). A postmodern perspective on learning organizations also allowed for an examination of the utility of continuous knowledge growth in learning organizations as a vehicle for adapting organizational structure to the emergence and expansion of diversity in society. Although it is unclear how the concept of the learning organization would reframe current thinking about diversity and leadership in higher education, one benefit to higher education from the postmodernist interfacing of learning and leadership frameworks is an emphasis on multilayered and multidimensional perspectives for conceiving of organizational culture as transformative (Kezar, 2000; Levin, 1998; Rosser, 2003; Whetten and Cameron, 1985). The emphasis on multilayered and multidimensional perspectives regarding leadership in higher education provides excellent opportunities for collectively envisioning the inclusive university of tomorrow as a learning organization. Although higher education organizational forms and practices remain rational bureaucratic in form, learning organization theories have taken the normative stage from those emphasizing bureaucratic hierarchical models. In this context, the transformation of higher education remains a major objective, and the impetus for including diversity as a core value of higher education complements the learning organization model.

Leadership in Higher Education

The study of leadership in higher education is rooted in theoretical and methodological orientations that address culture and climate issues in learning organizations. Studies of leadership in higher education reflect not only the influence of general theories of leadership from the social sciences but also perspectives developed to make sense of the rapid societal changes that have taken place over the past four decades. As such, the perspectives found in studies of leadership in higher education reflect a mix of market-based, postmodern, institutional, normative, social-identity, behavioral, and other emphases, spanning both private and public sectors (Cohen and March, 1986; Duryea, 2000; Peterson, 1985). At the methodological level are quantitative and qualitative areas of emphasis, each with a broad range of approaches reflecting a range of methodological orientations (see, for example, Peterson, Dill, and Mets, 1997; Rosser, 2003).

According to Trow (1985), leadership in higher education "is the taking of effective action to shape the character and direction of a college or university, presumably for the better" (p. 45). Although the definition is limited by its lack of emphasis on followers, it remains useful by allowing for the examination of factors internal to organizations and the relationship of organizations to their environments (for competing definitions of leadership, see Etzioni, 1965; Steers and Black, 1994). Similar to economic organizations in society, higher education has been greatly affected by technological and demographic changes in society. Massive demographic shifts in society have interjected issues of access, organizational climate, and leadership in higher education into the public eye (Carchidi and Peterson, 2000; Morris, 2005). Although the study of higher education has increased over the past several decades, not since the civil rights movement of the 1960s has higher education been surrounded by social and political struggles for access, equity, and inclusion. Calls for leadership focused on diversity are complemented by policies that increase the role of markets on higher education operations (see, for example, Bowen, Bok, and Burkhart, 1999).

Leadership in Higher Education

The sociological study of culture and its construction has long held that knowledge and its production are linked to social location in society (Sztompka, 1979). What one sees, how one frames issues, and the interests and values embodied in one's perspective are linked to one's membership in a group (including class) in society. Moreover, one can intentionally take the perspective of a particular group without assuming actual group membership to gain a deeper understanding of that group's interests and values (Tierney, 2001). This view of the epistemology of knowledge has been applied to the study of leadership in higher education with perceptions of leadership examined in relation to associated power conditions (Kezar, 2000). Leadership in higher education is defined and viewed differently by the different groups that make up the academy, with race, class, gender, and structural factors influencing the perceptions of constituents and the experiences of those who assume leadership roles (Minor and Tierney, 2005; Peterson and Spencer, 1990).

Different perceptions of leadership in higher education are found among administrators, faculty, staff, students, and other constituents (Bensimon, 1989a, 1989b; Bensimon, Neumann, and Birnbaum, 1989; Tierney, 1989a). Differences in perceptions of leadership also occur at the level of institutional stratification, with differences evident across the spectrum from two-year colleges to top-tier research institutions (Rosser, Johnsrud, and Heck, 2003). In many cases, empirical studies of perceptions of effective leadership in higher education are based on samples of staff and faculty members' perceptions of administrative leadership. In others, a more reflexive approach is used, with leaders providing their own perceptions of leadership in higher education (Tierney, 1989b, 2000; Wong and Tierney, 2001).

Leadership in higher education is a complex phenomenon with many dimensions and domains (Tierney, 1992). Presidents are expected to provide vision and administrative leadership and to work and communicate effectively on many different issues with governing boards, faculty, staff, students, parents, donors, and other constituents (Chaffee and Tierney, 1988). Fujita (1994) investigated the basis on which campus constituents assess presidential leadership and found substantial differences among governing board members, senior administrators, and faculty. These constituent groups work in different spheres in higher education and are positioned differently relative to the president. As a result, they tend to have different values, expectations, and experiences in relation to presidents. According to Fujita, differences between the constituent groups are most evident between governing board members and senior administrators on one hand, and faculty members on the other.

Board members and senior administrators, for instance, tend to accept the president as legitimate and competent, while faculty members tend to be more critical and are more likely to be disappointed relative to the sharing of power. Kerr and Gade (1986) note that faculty members tend to view most presidents as autocratic and evaluate their performance at "discounted rates." That is, their ratings of the performance of university presidents are usually lower than those of other constituent groups. Although this particular tension stems from the governance structure of institutions, it is not unlike the tensions that characterize intergroup and gender relations, which frame the social and cultural forms of domination that characterize campuses across the country.

Neumann (1988) studied faculty leadership by conducting interviews with thirty-one presidents and twenty-nine faculty leaders, mostly faculty senate leaders, at thirty-two institutions across the country. Respondents were asked to describe "good faculty leadership." The major finding of the study was that presidents and faculty differ considerably on what constitutes good faculty leadership. In general, faculty leadership tended to be seen from institutional and professional frameworks.

Those who saw faculty leadership from an institutional perspective tended to see good faculty leaders as those who put the institution rather than their own programmatic interests first. Those who saw faculty leadership from a professional perspective saw good faculty leaders as giving attention to academic activities (teaching, scholarship, and service). According to Neumann, presidents were more likely than faculty officers to view good faculty leadership as attending to traditional academic activities. Faculty leaders were more likely to emphasize faculty welfare and rights as primary areas of concern. These differences in perspective between presidents and faculty leaders were more evident at community and state colleges than at other types of institutions. Such factors as centralization, bureaucratization, and less regard for shared governance found at the lower end of the higher education spectrum may help explain these differences in perceptions. Neumann concluded that presidents and faculty leaders have substantially different views about what constitutes good faculty leadership.

Another important position of formal leadership in higher education is that of dean, a position that most often provides leadership for a college or school in a university. Studies on the leadership of deans have identified several domains of leadership, including the need to work effectively with constituents (Gallos, 2002; Morris, 1981). Rosser, Johnsrud, and Heck (2003), for instance, have identified seven leadership domains for academic deans: (1) vision and goal setting, (2) management of the unit, (3) interpersonal relationships, (4) communication skills, (5) research, professional, and community endeavors, (6) quality of the unit's education, and (7) support for institutional diversity. Similar to presidents and other academic leaders, deans have one foot firmly planted in the rational-bureaucratic structure of higher education and the other in the persuasive culture of shared governance. Because deans work with several constituent groups, they are also more likely to be seen differently across those groups. Faculty, for instance, expect that deans will communicate with different constituent groups and stakeholders, including faculty members and central administration, and garner the resources to maximize the potential of the faculty (Matczynski, Lasley, and Haberman, 1989).

Demographic characteristics also influence how leaders in higher education are perceived. According to Bray (2003), men and women differ in their perceptions of transgressions of administrative norms by deans. For instance, women tend to see inept evaluation and representation, unconveyed expectations, bending to pressure, public criticism, devaluing nonacademic staff, and disdain for faculty input as more inappropriate than do men. In addition, nonwhite faculty members are more likely than their white counterparts to find a dean's disdain for faculty input as inappropriate.

Definitions of leadership in higher education, as a result, are multidimensional and multilayered, shaped by demographic and structural factors. Leaders in higher education are expected to improve their organizations, engage in shared governance, abide by administrative norms, and communicate effectively with their constituents. From a postmodern perspective, leadership in higher education is a collective activity among organizational members, a social relationship that focuses on leading (Rost, 1993). As such, leadership in higher education is a vehicle for making organizational changes that reflect the mutual interests of organizational members (Rogers, 1992; Rost, 1991). Although observers may generally agree about what leaders should do, however, little agreement exists on what constitutes effective leadership in higher education (Pounder, 2001). In particular, even less agreement exists with regard to the association between effective leadership and goal setting for diversity initiatives. It is thus necessary to examine and discuss the nexus for diversity in the organizational culture of higher education.

Diversity and Organizational Culture

The normative view of the relationship between diversity and organizational culture holds that diversity is inherently good. For instance, diversity is good for "successful" business organizations that respond to a diverse environment by increasing the representation of racial and ethnic minorities at all organizational levels, contracting with minority suppliers, and using minority-owned investment banks (Colvin, 1999). Regarding the benefits of promoting diversity in higher education, Brown (2004) notes that promoting diversity in higher education creates a "culture of acceptance that fosters a sense of belonging among all persons by recognizing and respecting difference, and in so doing, promoting a sense of loyalty to the organization" (p. 29). Similarly,

Stadtman (1980) observes that promoting diversity in higher education offers a broad range of choices to learners, makes higher education nearly universally accessible, matches education to learning needs and skills, enables institutions to determine their own mission, and promotes institutional freedom and autonomy. In short, promoting diversity in higher education strengthens institutions by building on the opportunities for learning engendered by a diverse community; that is, it increases the success of higher education institutions.

Numerous studies have documented the benefits of diversity in higher education, with colleges and universities differing in purpose, form, decision-making processes, and degrees of shared governance and faculty professional autonomy (Baldridge, Curtis, Ecker, and Riley, 1977; Blau, 1973; Chesler, Lewis, and Crowfoot, 2005; Hurtado, Milem, Clayton-Pedersen, and Allen, 1999). Organizational views on diversity tend to emphasize competition, size, hierarchy, specialization, and environmental processes of natural selection (Birnbaum, 1983). Although the focus on diversity has been related to demographic and cultural factors in society, some concern exists that the focus on diversity in higher education is based on the cultural foundations of the dominant group—an obstacle to the promotion of cultural pluralism and diversity as core values of higher education (Chalmers, 1987; Lowe, 1999; Platt, 1993).

Challenges to Organizational Culture

Shifts in the organizational culture of higher education occurred as an outcome of struggles over civil rights in the 1960s and by population changes in society during the latter part of the twentieth century. The expansion of higher education in the 1950s and 1960s was a response to a mix of state and federal initiatives that intensified the demands on higher education for enhancing the representation of ethnic and racial minorities (Karen, 1991). According to Chang (2005), "The earliest initiatives to increase minority access on predominantly white campuses . . . . . .were prompted by desegregation mandates as well as social justice concerns grounded in the democratic principles of equal opportunity and equality" (p. 6). The entry of racial and ethnic minorities to higher education fueled a series of culture wars and raised questions about the cultural alignment of higher education with the needs of a culturally diverse society (Arthur and Shapiro, 1995).

The challenges facing higher education since the mid-twentieth century have demanded new concepts of leadership and leadership practices for institutions to realign or adapt themselves to an increasingly diverse environment. A watchword for a new leadership paradigm that emerged to meet the demands of the emergent global epoch is *transformation.* The expansion of globalization and its effect on social institutions have come to be seen as the transformation of society (Stiglitz, 1998). Transformation, unlike social change in general, is radical fundamental change that is the result of deliberate efforts by leaders and followers. As a result, transformational leadership is conceived as a type of leadership needed by organizations to respond and adapt to environmental change, that is, demographic and cultural diversity.

The need for transformational leadership in organizations was best articulated by Avolio, Waldman, and Yammarino (1991): "In a continually changing environment, the long range success of an organization depends on the ability of leadership at all levels to develop, stimulate and inspire followers. Transformational leaders—who offer individualized consideration, spark intellectual stimulation, provide inspirational motivation and engender idealized influence—should be understood and then developed" (p. 16). From a postmodern perspective, transformational leadership focuses on harnessing the energies of organizational participants to bring about organizational changes (Keough and Tobin, 2001).

Transformational Leadership and Diversity

According to Burns (1978), transformational leadership is capable of merging organizations with society in a manner that allows people to be self-reflexive and, as a result, able to actualize their interests. In addition, transformational leadership enables the organization to be seen as responding to the collective need for identity and commitment between persons and organizational culture. Yukl (1994), for example, argues that transformational leadership can be viewed as a "microlevel influence process between individuals and as a macrolevel process of mobilizing power to change social systems and reform institutions" (p. 351). That is, leadership is transformational because it motivates leaders to be visionaries that are able to transform organizational members into self-empowered leaders—into change agents (Kouzes and Posner, 1989; Tichy and Devanna, 1986).

Consider that diversity emerged from an unstable social and cultural environment as a challenge to higher education, especially to its organizational culture. Higher education institutions, like other institutions in society, faced significant objective and normative pressures to align themselves with rapidly changing cultural and demographic environmental conditions. In this context then, a new leadership paradigm was needed that could merge diversity with the transformation of higher education into an inclusive institution in American society. The transformation of higher education needed to include diversity as a core value if it was to increase the capacity of colleges and universities to prosper and keep pace with changes in the environment.

The Substance of Diversity Leadership in Higher Education

Transforming an organizational culture rooted in dominant group interests and conservative views about change has been a major challenge to leadership that seeks the inclusion of diversity in organizational culture. Tensions between administrators and faculty and between dominant and minority groups on campus combine at the intersection of structure and culture to produce a pattern in which presidents of institutions of higher education (and other formal leaders such as provosts and vice presidents) are more open to promoting diversity than are faculty members, who often actively resist making diversity a core value at their campuses (Lowe, 1999).

Matczynski, Lasley, and Haberman (1989), for example, in a survey of education research faculty (many of whom were former academic administrators) found that the capacity to develop and implement affirmative action plans was the least important of the qualities expected among deans, with ability to communicate effectively with diverse constituent groups ranking as the most important. Despite changing demographics and the increasing financial dependence of colleges and universities on minority enrollments, the majority of faculty members in American higher education continue to cast a blind eye to diversity as an important social force in their institutions (Jacobs, Cintron, and Canton, 2002; Smith, Altbach, and Lomotey, 2002; Turner and Myers, 2000). Consequently, diversity values and practices tend to remain at the margins of institutions of higher education.

Leadership in higher education that promotes the incorporation of diversity into organizational culture seeks the improvement of colleges and universities as a whole. Such leadership holds diversity as its core value and recognizes the need to transform higher education to meet the exigencies of a changing environment. Leadership focused on diversity envisions a multicultural environment at colleges and universities that is inclusive and respectful of the plurality of ethnic and racial groups in society. As such, it pursues a vision of colleges and universities as multicultural organizations seeking alignment with a rapidly changing society to meet the educational and research needs of all population segments in society.

In *Leadership Reconsidered,* Astin and Astin (2000) open a window through which one can observe how transformational leadership allows the organizational culture in higher education to respond to observable changes such as racial and ethnic diversity taking place in society. They argue that everyone can be a leader and seek to enlist college and university presidents, faculty members, student affairs personnel, and students in the betterment of higher education. To cope with the turbulence of change, they argue, leaders must possess new knowledge and skills and exhibit high levels of "emotional and spiritual wisdom and maturity" (Astin and Astin, 2000, p. 1). They prescribe a collaborative approach to leadership over that of hierarchical power and authority. Interestingly, an institution once governed by a collegial structure, by slowly adopting (or succumbing to) the rational-bureaucratic model of industrial organizations, has become constrained in its capacity to adapt to rapid changes in society.

Today's institutions of higher education reflect the patterns of social stratification in society and serve as the contexts in which intergroup struggles and leadership take place. Situated in much more fractured ideological discourses than those surrounding technology and economic restructuring, institutions of higher education are focal points for struggles between dominant and racial and ethnic minority groups in society. Politically, the context for leadership in higher education has changed considerably over the past four decades. As a result, the role of a president has shifted from leading for academic values to one managing public relations and fundraising campaigns; ironically, the length of tenure in office has decreased significantly. Davis and Davis (1999) note, for example, that the average length of tenure for university presidents at state and land-grant institutions decreased from seven to four years between 1965 and 1997—in sharp contrast to the "unfragmented presidency" of the early twentieth century that not only combined the functions of vice president positions common at most colleges and universities but also allowed presidents to serve for several years (Ogilvy, 1963). As the complexity of higher education organizations has increased, challenges facing higher education leaders have also increased, especially the need for continuing development in the area of diversity (Borkowski, 1988; Collins and Johnson, 1988).

Like leadership in other societal spheres, diversity leadership in higher education occurs through complex relationships in and across groups in contexts of structured inequalities that are part of this nation's history. Class, gender, race, and culture influence and are embodied in the dynamics of leadership in higher education and the struggles over strategic changes and directions that take place. These factors affect leadership as objective factors and as part of the conceptual frameworks used to examine patterns of leadership in higher education.

Positioning Diversity Leadership in Higher Education

Leadership that addresses diversity issues and concerns in higher education is highly multidimensional and complex. Substantively, it is much more than a simple response or adaptation to demographic representation:—it is about the intergroup dynamics that characterize colleges and universities in both structure and culture. Leadership that addresses diversity issues and concerns in higher education is identified as *diversity leadership*. Diversity leadership uses primary organizational dimensions such as competition and success to incorporate diverse people or groups and enhance the organizational success in a changing environment (Winston, 2001). As noted earlier, the public and stakeholders in higher education not only recognize the importance of diversity in higher education, but also support initiatives that would implement diversity in organizational practices. In a sense, diversity leadership is about power and authority and how widely they are shared across the plurality of people and groups that have systematically been excluded from full participation (Chen and Vilsor, 1996).

We conceive of diversity leadership, then, as an organizational tool for responding and adapting to changes in the environment from which institutions of higher education recruit members and participants. We also conceive of diversity leadership as nested in organizational roles and practices that promote changes in higher education's organizational culture as it responds to diversity in racial and ethnic minority populations. From a more optimistic perspective, diversity leadership signals higher education's "improved capacity to educate in a pluralistic society for a pluralistic world" (Smith, 2000, p. 532). Thus, diversity leadership has the potential to alter organizational culture by promoting leadership roles and practices from the perspective of diversity.

Challenges for Diversity Leadership

Today the overwhelming majority of private liberal arts and public colleges and universities in this country maintain organizational values, processes, and practices that favor members of the dominant group, that is, white Americans, especially men. Diversity leadership seeks to combine elements of a new leadership paradigm with an emphasis on transformation, with the values of cultural pluralism and multiculturalism transforming colleges and universities into inclusive organizations that embody diversity as a core value and emphasize respect for the plurality of population groups that make up campus communities. Battin (1997) argues that for higher education to survive in a changing environment, it must meet two obligations, diversity and leadership: "diversity because it is not only morally right, but also demographically smart as the traditional talent pool continues to shrink; and the assurance of leadership succession to guide our institutions through a confusing transformational period in which there is no longer a stable, bureaucratic structure to compensate for lack of leadership" (p. 16).

Racial and ethnic minorities in higher education have had to play by the rules of the dominant status group—white males. Consequently, racial and ethnic minorities have felt like outsiders, seldom feeling accepted and respected for their differences (except perhaps as exotic objects that attract the occasional interest of members of the dominant group) (Chesler, Lewis, and Crowfoot, 2005; Johnsrud and Sadao, 1998). As is the case in every organization, the dominant group seeks to maintain its position in the organization by protecting the culture that provides it with status and privilege (Dunham, 2002; Hays, 2000; Wood, 2000). The result is a constant, though not always overt, struggle over organizational change between racial and ethnic minorities on the one hand and dominant group members on the other. These lines of struggle are permeable, and members of the different groups sometimes cross back and forth, depending on specific issues at any particular time (Alderfer and Thomas, 1988; Nkomo, 1992).

In this context of struggle, diversity is perceived differently and usually in accordance with the vested interests of campus members and the groups of which they are a part (see the previous chapter). Because colleges and universities reflect the culture and values of the dominant group, great emphasis is placed on rational processes and on co-opting or managing diversity (Aguirre and Martinez, 2003b). One of the primary approaches organizations take toward their external environments is that of co-opting those features that pose problems or threats to their existence (Selznick, 1948). For example, one outcome of the effective management of diversity is that organizations "benefit from diversity efforts by cutting personnel costs, which have become a major expense for most organizations. The claim is that effective diversity practices and policies will reduce the number of expensive discrimination complaints . . ." (Baker, 1996, p. 147).

For example, the practice of tokenism still evident in higher education is intended to incorporate demographic diversity in the existing normative structure of authority as a way of showing that the organization embodies diversity as a value (Contreras, 1998). The intent is to co-opt the threat of diversity without the organization's having to change itself to fit the changing environment. Another approach used by organizations is to promote organizational effectiveness by harnessing diversity in the enhancement of productivity. In higher education, one of the major indicators of productivity is student enrollment, which usually means using diversity to attract diverse students: "look, there are others like you here."

Colleges and universities often engage in impression management and portray themselves, sometimes unethically, as diverse organizations through brochures, Web pages, and other materials used to recruit students. In this manner, colleges and universities can claim to be serving all population groups at the same time they compete for diverse students, yet they have not actually transformed themselves into diverse institutions. For example, the University of Wisconsin at Madison was criticized for doctoring a photograph by inserting a black student's face into a crowd of white Badger football fans. University officials used the doctored photograph on the cover of the university's undergraduate application booklet to show diversity in the student population (Durhams, 2000).

In seeking to manage diversity, colleges and universities not only remain in their rational approach to their external environment but also inhibit effectiveness and fail to serve the nation as a whole. Diversity leadership goes beyond the rational approach to co-opting and managing diversity. It does so by recognizing and valuing the different cultural groups in the external environment and creating learning and workplace environments that integrate these cultural groups as integral elements of the organizational culture in higher education. As Ibarra (2001) has noted, "The central conflict regarding campus diversity and demographic change is between culturally different populations and traditional academic values—those that involve how things are done in academia. Now the pressures for change—the incentives—are mounting" (p. 10).

Summary

Despite the public perception that diversity signals a "new cultural diversity" in U.S. society, one must not ignore the possibility that diversity remains a hidden dimension in the social and organizational structure of American society. The increasing racial and ethnic diversity that is transforming the complexion of U.S. society remains unrepresented in American society's institutions of higher education. Despite observable changes in the racial and ethnic complexion of U.S. society, diversity remains hidden and mostly unwelcome in the organizational culture of higher education. As we have noted in this chapter, the organizational culture in higher education resists the inclusion of diversity because it requires a major transformation to the structuring of leadership roles and practices in higher education.

If diversity is an unwelcome guest hidden behind the door in American higher education, then how does one discuss its nexus with leadership concerns in higher education? From the onset, one must acknowledge that a discussion of the nexus for diversity and leadership in higher education is hampered by conceptual and definitional issues in its organizational culture. First, diversity is a social phenomenon that is associated with populations and persons located on the margins of mainstream society. That is, diversity is linked to the structural position of racial and ethnic minority persons in society, a structural position shaped by social forces that marginalize and exclude persons in society.

The increased number, especially in the last two decades, of racial and ethnic minority persons in the U.S. population has made them more noticeable on the margins of society (sometimes highlighted by natural disasters such as Hurricane Katrina). By sheer numbers they have become more visible, and indirectly, their increased numbers have highlighted their absence in general from social and economic organizations in mainstream society. Hence, American society is perceived as becoming more diverse, which in turn creates the perception that social institutions need to respond to the increasing diversity in society. In a sense, diversity in American society has become visible because the margins of society have become more noticeable through the increased numbers of racial and ethnic minorities. As a result, a dilemma for a discussion of the nexus for diversity and leadership in higher education is that diversity is perceived as an issue associated with marginal persons in society instead of being perceived as a social force that signals the need to broaden the boundaries of the mainstream to be more inclusive.

One challenge to a discussion of the nexus for diversity and leadership in the organizational culture of higher education is hampered by the absence of diversity from social and economic organizations in American society. One outcome of its absence is that one is not able to observe comparative leadership models for the transformative qualities of diversity in organizations. Because diversity is missing from social organizations, one is unable to observe the synergistic relationship between diversity and organizational structure. In particular, one is unable to observe how organizations have transformed themselves to fit diversity in their structure and culture. Ironically, the literature on organizational leadership offers limited insights regarding the fit of diversity in organizational structure because the literature has taken very little notice of race and ethnicity as social forces in organizational design. From an organizational perspective, one is unable to observe how organizations have responded to the fit of diversity in their structure because one is unable to evaluate organizational responses to diversity.

We have suggested in this chapter that the little attention that diversity has attracted as a social force in organizational studies reflects the operation of an assumption that organizations are relatively homogeneous structures regarding the racial and ethnic makeup of their members, namely, that organizational members are white. Institutions of higher education in the United States remain predominantly white institutions that promote and maintain cultural values and orientations rooted in the dominant group's interests (see, for example, Chan and Wang, 1991; Colon, 1991; Hale, 2004). The assumption that organizations are relatively homogeneous structures turns diversity into a descriptive measure rather than a social force pregnant with change. As a descriptive measure, diversity is treated only as representing shifts in the racial and ethnic makeup of American society. As a social force, diversity is regarded as a vehicle for transforming the organizational character of society to mirror its racial and ethnic makeup. The challenge for higher education is to treat diversity as a social force by using diversity leadership to transform higher education's organizational culture.

Finally, a discussion of the nexus for diversity and leadership in higher education is hampered by the manner in which one defines leadership. For example, the general definition of leadership found in the organizational literature is focused on promoting and maintaining compliance among organizational participants. In addition, definitions of leadership too often stress power relations between the organizational structure and participants' behavior; leadership involves the capacity to influence others to do something they might not otherwise do themselves. In the process, the leader must also make people believe that they want or choose to do something they would not do on their own. So how do these views of leadership challenge a discussion of the nexus for diversity and leadership in higher education?

On the one hand, a person's ability to influence others is directly related to his or her position in a hierarchy in society. For the purpose of discussion, the hierarchy we focus on is rooted in racial and ethnic inequality (see Chesler, Lewis, and Crowfoot, 2005; Law, Phillips and Turney, 2004). Given the historical patterns of privilege in American society, white people tend to occupy the majority of positions toward the top end of the hierarchy, whereas ethnic and racial minority persons tend to occupy the majority of positions toward the bottom end of the hierarchy. If one's position in the hierarchy is associated with one's ability to lead others, then it is likely that white persons will occupy leadership roles in society. From another point of view, given their position in the hierarchy it is unlikely that racial and ethnic minority persons will occupy leadership roles in society. These two statements contextualize the general observation that one is more likely to find white people than racial and ethnic minorities in leadership roles.

On the other hand, leadership is a form of power, a power tied to the ability to cause change in another person's social or behavioral orientations. Implicit is the assumption that, all things being equal between persons, leadership can find expression as one person's being able to influence or lead another person. What does "all things being equal" mean? Basically it means that people in the same social or organizational context share similar if not the same interpersonal characteristics. For our purpose, it means that leadership is assumed to revolve around the interpersonal relations characterizing white people and not those of racial and ethnic minorities. In a sense then, the expression of leadership has become identified with and embedded in white interpersonal relations.

Diversity leadership, as a result, may not be compatible with organizational culture, especially in higher education. Leadership assumes that a high index of homogeneity will be present among organizational members for leadership to find expression, whereas diversity is a social force that challenges homogeneity in organizational culture. How then do institutions of higher education mediate the synergistic relationship between diversity and leadership in their organizational culture? The challenge of diversity leadership to organizational culture in higher education is to use the centrality of leadership to organizational integrity while incorporating diversity as an emergent dimension in organizational design.

Diversity and Organizational Leadership in Higher Education

JUSTICE O'CONNOR IN HER OPINION REGARDING *GRUTTER* noted that in twenty-five years the use of racial preferences would no longer be necessary for promoting student diversity in higher education. One might ask, Will racial preferences no longer be necessary because higher education will achieve a race-neutral organizational culture? Or will higher education promote leadership practices that are inclusive of diversity instead of tools for remediating an exclusionary organizational culture for diversity? Although one might interpret Justice O'Connor's observation as having implications only for student diversity in higher education, the observation she makes is rooted in an implicit assumption that organizational leadership changes in higher education will result in the elimination of racial preferences. As a result, Justice O'Connor's observation suggests that organizational leadership in higher education will undergo a transformation in the next twenty-five years that will transcend the use of institutional initiatives specifically targeting diversity. In particular, her observation suggests that diversity will be the driving social force for changing the institutional fabric of society, resulting in more inclusive organizational structures for diverse populations.

The purpose of this chapter is to discuss and examine leadership models associated with diversity initiatives in higher education to assess the relative effectiveness of organizational strategies focused on diversity. In particular, we examine diversity leadership models in higher education that tend to produce positive results. One purpose for examining diversity leadership models in this chapter is to construct a conceptual framework that can guide organizational strategies in the twenty-first century. From a general perspective, efforts to reframe institutions of higher education to be more inclusive of diversity have moved from social movement to learning organizational strategies, or what we call the "rationalization of social movement strategies"—the use of strategic planning mechanisms for managing strategic organizational change (see, for example, Tyack and Hansot, 1980). The following two questions serve as guides for discussion in this chapter:

What is the context for diversity in organizational leadership in higher education?

How does incorporating diversity into organizational leadership allow institutions of higher education to respond to increasing diversity in society?

The emphasis in this chapter is on a discussion of conceptual issues and frameworks that are linked with the use of organizational strategies focused on diversity in higher education. Whereas the previous chapter focused on organizational culture, this chapter focuses on process by examining competing organizational responses to diversity, such as the difference between co-optive and transformative organizational responses. By *process,* we mean the manner in which organizational strategies in higher education are used to respond to diversity. We start our discussion in this chapter by reviewing the introduction of business organization models focused on diversity to higher education. We then discuss the use of competing organizational strategies focused on diversity—for example, co-optation versus transformation—in higher education. After that, we provide an overview of the social and demographic changes that created the nexus for diversity strategies in higher education. In particular, we discuss how diversity strategies in higher education are important for the adaptation of organizational culture to increased demands in society for (diversity) representation in higher education.

Leadership Models and Frameworks in Higher Education

According to Hall (1996), leadership is often treated in organizations as an easy solution to problems such as "inappropriate structural arrangements, power distributions that block effective actions, lack of resources, archaic procedures, and other, more basic organizational problems" (p. 139). If the lack of diversity in its leadership roles and practices is perceived as a challenge for an organization, then one would expect the organization to respond by diversifying its leadership to deal with the challenge. Consequently, we argue that the challenge for higher education is to implement diversity in its organizational culture by transforming organizational structure. For example, Brayboy (2003) has noted that implementing diversity in higher education is a challenge because "predominantly white institutions of higher education often view diversity as a freestanding policy . . . that diversity is something that can be implemented without necessarily changing the underlying structure of the institution and its day-to-day operations" (p. 73).

Business organizations in the United States are often used as prototypical models for higher education regarding strategies for responding to the needs and concerns of diversity (Allison, 1999; Bond and Pyle, 1998). Despite the efforts of business organizations to respond to diversity, they often find themselves in the spotlight for failing to respond effectively to diversity issues such as providing opportunities for racial and ethnic minorities to assume leadership roles (Jacobs, 2002). For example, in 2000, Coca-Cola settled a class-action lawsuit initiated by black workers who claimed they were denied equal pay, promotions, and opportunity to apply for executive positions. The settlement cost Coca-Cola $192.5 million. Four years earlier, in 1996, Texaco agreed to pay $176 million in a similar lawsuit. As a result, the failure of business organizations to respond appropriately and effectively to diversity has had a noticeable cost on organizational resources—namely, money. Interestingly, higher education institutions have proposed using the framework of "multiple intelligences" to prepare business students for working in a diverse workforce and for enhancing their ability to recognize the organizational benefits of diversity (Martin, 2003). For instance, in the previous chapter we observed that business organizations responded to diversity by developing strategies that sought to "manage diversity" to buffer themselves from environmental demands (Baker, 1996).

Regarding a business organization's need to respond to diversity, Ramirez (2000) notes that "embracing diversity means implementing organizational systems and practices to manage people so that the potential advantages of diversity are maximized and disadvantages are minimized" (p. 132). In other words, business organizations must respond to diversity by seeking to develop practices that maximize advantages associated with diversity while minimizing disadvantages. The two principal components to diversity in economic organizations are thus advantages and disadvantages.

If Hall's observation is valid that leadership is often viewed as an easy solution to organizational problems, then leadership practices in business organizations may be a response to what the organization identifies as the advantages of diversity. That is, diversity is treated as an organizational problem, but by focusing on its advantages, its problematic character is defused and organizations are able to position themselves to reap the benefits of diversity. One can assume that the advantages of diversity to business organizations are those enabling an organization to pursue its goals in a rational manner. As such, diversity is something to be subsumed into the rational, goal-seeking activity of the organization and not as a social force in organizational structure.

Perhaps the most common, if not most appropriate, strategy for a business organization to pursue in its response to diversity in society is to introduce diversity in its leadership practices. Frequently, the intent on the part of organizations that pursue this strategy is to have diverse leadership without having to alter the interpersonal relations surrounding leadership practices. In a sense, diverse leadership serves the rational, goal-seeking design of the organization without having the organizational structure altered to fit diversity. For example, a survey of thirty-five major U.S. corporations conducted by Korn/Ferry International, an executive development and recruitment company, found that corporate executives regard institutional arrangements, such as mentoring and leadership programs with minority-oriented organizations, as effective vehicles for cultivating talent among minority professionals (Lewis, 2002).

From an organizational perspective, mentoring programs are a rational means for introducing diversity into organizational leadership that is aligned with organizational goals, especially if one considers that mentoring programs do not strain organizational or financial resources. The focus is on adapting diversity to organizational structure. For example, business organizations have addressed diversity issues by linking with business schools in higher education for the preparation of racial and ethnic minority group members that can develop and implement plans for a business organization's response to diversity (Sappal, 2003; Williamson, 2000).

From a social-psychological perspective, mentoring programs increase the likelihood that diverse organizational members, especially those in leadership roles, will identify with the organization (Alderfer, 1985). As a result, diverse identities in organizational structures may not serve persons as tools for promoting strategies or practices that result in organizational change. In more general language, business organizations recruit racial and ethnic minority people to exhibit practices in leadership positions that are congruent with organizational structure, thus constraining them from using their self-identification with diversity as a tool for changing organizational structure. A similar process occurs in higher education (see Martinez, 2005).

Another approach to bringing diversity to leadership in organizations is to use organizational resources to establish institutional arrangements that socialize diverse populations to assume roles in the organization. For example, the Higher Education Forum was formed in January 2000 from a coalition of twenty-five corporations, thirty-six universities, and seven nonprofit organizations (Merritt, 2002). According to some of the forum's members, the "audience is growing more diverse, so the communities we serve benefit if our employees are racially and ethnically diverse" (p. 56). The forum uses financial aid programs to assist minority students in their pursuit of a college education. Specifically, the forum is interested in increasing minority student college enrollments in business fields. By using financial incentives such as scholarships and paid internships, the forum focuses on steering minority students to undergraduate business programs that can in turn track them into MBA programs. The result is a supply of minority people socialized to assume work roles in economic organizations—corporate roles that require a corporate identity in which diversity is a static and descriptive characteristic. In a sense, the forum is a problematic example of diversity because, although it seeks to promote diversity in organizational structure, it does not promote diversity as a social force capable of transforming organizational culture.

Institutions of higher education have adopted practices from business organizations to promote diversity in organizational leadership. For example, institutions of higher education have responded to the need to implement initiatives that mentor racial and ethnic minorities in leadership positions by forming partnerships with professional organizations and philanthropic foundations that offer a variety of resources on leadership development from annual conferences and workshops to yearlong and multiyear development programs (Leon, 2005). Some of the initiatives focus on development institutes for new senior administrators, continuing professional development programs for senior administrators, and development programs for midlevel administrators in senior administrative positions. The following programs provide leadership development opportunities in the area of higher education:

American Association of Community Colleges, Future Leaders Institute

American Association of Medical Colleges, Faculty Development and Leadership

American Association of State Colleges and Universities, Millennium Leadership Initiative

American Association of University Women Leadership and Training Institute

American Council on Education, ACE Fellows Program

American Council on Education/Office of Women in Higher Education, National and Regional Leadership Forums

American Indian Higher Education Consortium Leadership Fellows Program

Association for Biblical Higher Education, Leadership Development for Biblical Higher Education

Association of Colleges and Research Libraries/Harvard Leadership Institute for Academic Librarians

Committee on Institutional Cooperation, CIC Academic Leadership Program

Council for Graduate Schools, Preparing Future Faculty Program

Harvard University, Institute for Management and Leadership in Education

Higher Education Resource Service, HERS Management Institute for Women in Higher Education Administration

Higher Education Staff Development Agency, Leadership and Management Development

Hispanic Association of Colleges and Universities, HACU Kellogg Leadership
　Fellows Program

Leadership Education for Asian Pacifics, Inc., Leadership Development for
　Higher Education Program

Leadership Foundation for Higher Education, Developing Tomorrow's Leaders

National Association for Equal Opportunity in Higher Education Kellogg
　Leadership Fellows Program

National Forum on Higher Education for the Public Good, Intergenerational
　Scholars Symposia

W. K. Kellogg Foundation, Kellogg Minority Serving Institutions Leadership
　Fellows Program

Although institutions of higher education have used programmatic initiatives such as those listed above to promote diversity, these initiatives often have not resulted in organizational frameworks for implementing diversity in organizational leadership. How then do institutions of higher education develop frameworks for promoting diversity that meet the challenge of organizational leadership? Bowen, Bok, and Burkhart (1999) suggest that institutions of higher education would improve their chances of incorporating diversity in organizational practices if they borrowed ideas or models from business organizations in their efforts promoting diversity. Jackson (2006), for example, suggests that human resource practices and policies in higher education institutions can be analyzed to see the impact they have on racial and ethnic minorities. Business organizations analyze their human resource practices and policies to examine their effect on the accommodation and incorporation of racial and ethnic minority groups, especially underrepresentation (Byrkjeflot and Fligstein, 1996). Similarly, institutions of higher education can examine their human resource policies and practices to examine how they can accommodate racial and ethnic minorities in organizational leadership. Specifically, how can human resource policies and practices promote diversity without being perceived as a threat to the organizational culture?

From another perspective, Taylor (1995) argues that to promote diversity in organizational leadership, "outmoded traditions of leadership and dated administrative paradigms need to be deconstructed" (p. 63), and "leaders must find ways to challenge static notions of equality, opportunity, and fairness, in themselves and their staff" (p. 66). A paradigm that incorporates diversity in organizational leadership would have some of the following characteristics: (1) commitment to equity, access, and excellence; (2) recognition that racial and ethnic minorities have a place in knowledge production; (3) promotion of cultural pluralism; and (4) support of democratic principles and the recognition of racial and ethnic minorities in the national culture. As such, leaders can be change agents who transform the organizational culture to reflect the pluralistic and democratic character of American society. To be effective change agents in higher education, leaders must "situate themselves in a larger historical narrative of this country . . . [and be able to] grasp the complex dynamics of our peoplehood and imagine a future grounded in the best of our past" (West, 1994, p. 13). Thus, incorporating diversity in organizational leadership is more than just adopting organizational practices sensitive to diversity. It requires the construction of frameworks for leadership in higher education that are visionary in promoting the pluralistic character in American society.

Leadership as Contested Terrain in Higher Education

Higher education is contested terrain where intergroup struggles between the dominant group and minority groups are played out similar to the manner in which they express themselves in society (Chesler, Lewis, and Crowfoot, 2005; Conrad, 1978; Leatherman, 1993). More important, higher education is contested terrain characterized by social relations where groups in privileged positions on campus seek to retain their status, while groups in subordinate or marginal positions seek to create a more just distribution of opportunities and rewards (Agathangelou and Zalewski, 2005; Chang, Witt, Jones, and Hakuta, 2003; Hoover, 2002). The introduction of diversity initiatives in higher education intensifies the struggle between dominant and minority groups over access to a valued resource such as a college degree. In particular, dominant groups perceive diversity as the imposition of difference in the institutional environment and as a threat to quality in the distribution of education opportunities. The purpose of leadership in higher education then is to promote social justice principles that promote diversity as a transformative force in higher education and as a social change agent in society (Arocena and Sutz, 2005). As Mabokela and Madsen (2003) note, "Leaders who seek to create a community of difference will have to develop an understanding of power and control and recognize the need to negotiate and accommodate norms and shared purposes of both majority and minority groups" (p. 132).

Aguirre and Martinez (2002) argue that higher education has been reluctant to embrace diversity as a core value and as a "necessary dimension toward building themselves into inclusive organizations" (p. 53). It does not mean that diverse groups have not made any gains in creating multicultural learning and working environments in America's colleges and universities. Clearly, colleges and universities have changed considerably since the civil rights movement of the 1960s, including expanded access, broader curricula, and more inclusive environments (Association of American Colleges and Universities, n.d.; Richardson and Skinner, 1991). But higher education remains contested terrain where, as Frederick Douglass observed more than a century ago about U.S. society—power concedes nothing without demands and struggles (Kohn, 2005; Moss, 2004).

Unsurprisingly, efforts to transform America's colleges and universities into diverse organizations have been nested in intergroup struggles over discrimination and social justice in society (Banks, 1995; Chesler, Lewis, and Crowfoot, 2005). The struggle over discrimination and social justice inside and outside institutions of higher education has turned American college and university campuses into contested terrain where cultural and political battles continue to take place (Essed, 2004). In addition, deindustrialization and the economic restructuring of the past several decades have created conditions of relatively scarce resources that have intensified the struggles over diversity involving discrimination and social justice and have pitted diversity against pressures for institutional efficiency and accountability (American Association of University Women, 2005; Galis, 1993; Tebbs and Turner, 2005).

Responding to Struggles over Diversity

Generally, institutions of higher education have responded to the struggles over discrimination and social justice linked with diversity issues by practicing co-optation versus transformation strategies. In his classic study of the Tennessee Valley Authority, Selznick (1949) coined the word *co-optation* to illustrate how public programs designed to change social structure often result in greater benefits for those in a position to design the public programs than for the intended beneficiaries of the programs (Jurik, Blumenthal, Smith, and Portillos, 2000; O'Toole and Meier, 2003). According to Selznick (1949), co-optation is the "process of absorbing new elements into the leadership or policy determining structure of an organization as a means of averting threats to its stability or existence" (p. 34). In higher education, for example, Brayboy (2003) identifies the use of co-optation strategies to address discrimination and social justice issues linked to diversity as "offer new courses on diversity, hire a few faculty of color, assign these faculty to cover committee assignments, work with students of color, serve as role models, and offer helpful suggestions on how to be a more user-friendly institution to all the students, including the ones of color" (p. 73). The purpose of co-optation strategies is to use diversity dimensions in the organizational culture—minority faculty, multiculturalism in the curriculum, and role models for minority students—as buffers to protect organizational culture rather than change it (Aguirre, 2005).

The notion of transformational strategies emerged in business organizations as an effort to be more competitive in a rapidly expanding global society (Conger, 1999). Transformation was conceptualized as a process in the organizational culture for developing adaptive strategies that responded to social and demographic changes in the environment without necessarily changing the whole organization. In this sense, transformational strategies allow an organization to overcome resistance to change in certain aspects of its organizational culture. In higher education, transformational strategies identify "common goals and objectives . . . [that] . . . make it possible . . . to induce creativity, productivity, and/or internal organizational change, even in unfavorable university-wide climates" (Bess and Goldman, 2001, p. 436). Transformational strategies in higher education seek to create an "environment that will encourage a socialization and learning process that adequately prepares students for an increasingly diverse society" (Judkins and LaHurd, 1999, p. 789).

Co-optation Versus Transformation Strategies

Although no one approach has been entirely successful, co-optation and transformation strategies have resulted in compromises and concessions among the plurality of groups that constitute campus communities. What are the implications of each type of strategy for leadership focused on diversity in higher education? In general, co-optation strategies stem from a rational-bureaucratic approach for managing organizations that promotes the dominant group's ideological and vested interests in higher education. As such, co-optation strategies promote leadership practices that seek to fit diversity in the organizational culture in higher education; that is, the goal is to change diversity to fit the dominant group's interests. In contrast, transformational strategies respond to the demands for social justice regarding the incorporation of racial and ethnic minorities in the institutional fabric of society. As such, transformation strategies promote leadership practices that seek to change the organizational culture to incorporate diversity by challenging the dominant group's resistance to diversity.

The rational-bureaucratic approach to diversity in organizations makes two important assumptions: (1) organizations are homogeneous (Hooijberg and DiTomaso, 1996), and (2) features of the environment that threaten to destabilize an organization are to be co-opted as part of the organization's adjustment to the changing environment (Selznick, 1948). These assumptions provide the foundation for organizational leadership strategies that treat diversity as a descriptive feature of the organization, as opposed to treating it as a core element (Aguirre and Martinez, 2003b). American higher education organizations, like other institutions in society, seek to control diversity as an emergent feature of the environment as they pursue the realization of their missions in accordance with the core values of efficiency and effectiveness. Following the rationale-bureaucratic model, for example, Ingle (2005) suggests that campus diversity initiatives should be implemented in a manner similar to a capital campaign to assess the effectiveness of the campus's strategic focus on managing diversity. One result would be that campus leadership would seek to manage diversity to reflect the institution's mission statement rather than changing it to incorporate diversity.

Co-optation strategies also seek to maintain monocultural environments in which racial and ethnic minorities participate in restricted roles in the dominant white patriarchal order of organizations. Aguirre and Martinez (2002) argue that leadership focused on diversity in this context is stagnant, stripped of its potential to transform institutional culture and pedagogical practices in higher education, and limited to episodic, highly visible displays during special occasions (such as accreditation or trustee visits) when it is important to promote an institutional image of diversity. Similarly, Pavel (2003) argues that leadership supportive of co-optation diversity initiatives is often not enough to create a campus environment in which multiculturalism enhances student learning; instead, it is perceived as a superficial response to diversity and educational inequality.

In comparison, transformation strategies seek to increase higher education's readiness to transform itself into a diverse organization. The aim is to enhance higher education's recognition of diversity issues by engaging campus community members in responding to social justice demands from racial and ethnic minorities, demographic shifts in society, and the promotion of multiculturalism in the organizational climate and culture (Haro, 1992; Niemann and Maruyama, 2005; Winston, 2001). Leadership practices, for instance, that focus on organizational transformation emphasize accommodation to and tolerance for racial and ethnic minorities, with diversity "awareness" programs required to alter organizational culture (Brandt, 1994; Sandham, 1997). The transformation process in institutions of higher education seeks to manage differences in the organizational culture and reduce social distance between the dominant group and minority groups. One purpose for transforming the organizational culture in higher education is to promote difference as a vehicle for building on the strengths brought about from incorporating diversity as a core value in the organizational culture, especially in an organizational culture rooted in monocultural values and social practices (Denton, 1997; Higgs, 1996).

Leadership practices focused on transforming organizational culture thus allow higher education to promote a vision of diversity that is engaging, educational, and an improvement in the organization's quality of life. Diversity is emphasized as a core value in the organizational culture, and proactive measures are employed to promote the development of a diverse organization; achievements in promoting diversity are recognized and rewarded in the higher education organization (Chang, 2002). Diversity leadership practices in higher education promote diverse norms in the organizational culture to change behaviors, assumptions, policies, and social practices that favor the dominant group by limiting the access of racial and ethnic minorities to valued resources and roles (Bower, 2002; Brown, 2004; Lowe, 1999; Niemann and Dovidio, 1998). In general, rather than changing diversity (in the form of racial and ethnic minorities) to fit into the organizational culture, diversity leadership practices in higher education transform organizational culture to incorporate social practices, values, and assumptions that foster diversity.

Despite perceptions among members of the dominant group that racial and ethnic minorities receive privileged treatment in higher education, ethnic and racial minorities continue to experience second-class membership in institutions of higher education (Aguirre, 2000; Fenelon, 2003; Turner, 2003). Members of the dominant group in higher education continue to resist change by using the power they hold in the organizational culture of higher education and the power of the courts when they challenge the constitutionality of diversity initiatives such as affirmative action, which is itself a mechanism reflecting the a co-optation strategy for organizational development (Aguirre and Martinez, 2003a; Garcia, 2000; Niemann and Dovidio, 2005; Padilla and Martinez, 2005).

The resistance of the dominant group's members to affirmative action in the admissions process, for example, persisted throughout the 1990s and has continued into the twenty-first century, even after the U.S. Supreme Court's decision affirmed diversity as a compelling societal interest in *Grutter* in 2003 (Green, 2004). Despite the Court's ruling in *Grutter,* the Center for Individual Rights continued to push *Smith* v. *University of Washington Law School,* a case in which the Ninth Circuit Court upheld the law school's policies at the time, until the U.S. Supreme Court declined for a second time to hear the case in 2005. As a result, higher education remains contested terrain in which progress moving from exclusive and monocultural institutions of the last century to diverse and multicultural institutions is limited by contexts of adversity and intergroup struggles (Chesler, Lewis, and Crowfoot, 2005; Gurin, Lehman, and Lewis, 2004).

The Nexus for Diversity Leadership Strategies

Diversity-oriented change in higher education has occurred unevenly in and across institutions because the dominant group feels threatened and actively seeks to maintain its privileged position and because institutions of higher education are rule bound and focused on maintaining a homeostatic environment and culture (Bass, 1985). Although each institution of higher education has its own organizational culture that constrains or facilitates change in relation to diversity, changes may occur at several organizational levels. Institutions of higher education can ignore or embrace diversity at each level, but leadership has tended to target each of them for changes (Bess and Goldman, 2001; Chesler, Lewis, and Crowfoot, 2005). In contrast, leadership in business organizations targets the overall organizational structure for fostering diversity (Foldy, 2004; Winston, 2001).

Leadership strategies that promote diversity in higher education tend to champion alliances focused on changing specific aspects in the institutional environment. According to Benjamin (1996), diversity initiatives promoted on college campuses in the 1960s and early 1970s were responses to changes in the political climate in society and focused on the recruitment and admission of minority students and the creation of minority-specific curriculum programs. These changes resulted in academic support programs for minority students, the recruitment of minority faculty, diversity training programs, diversity course requirements, and institutional diversity plans (Hubbard, 1998). Efforts in each of these areas were met with resistance to change; the dominant group often regarded diversity gains and achievements as attacks on institutional integrity (Ibarra, 2001; Justiz, Wilson, and Bjork, 1994; Losco and Fife, 2000).

With changes in the political climate in society and in the racial and ethnic composition of student populations across the United States during the 1970s, institutions of higher education responded on two levels: (1) expanding curriculum programs through the creation of black, Chicano, Native American, and Asian American studies; and (2) providing academic support and mentoring programs for racial and ethnic minority students (Butler and Walter, 1991; Calderon and Saldivar, 1991; Colon, 2003; Padeken and Stein, 2003). The first was a compromise—a response to the civil rights movement that pressured higher education to change. The second was part of higher education's response to the expansion of higher education that began in the period following World War II and was part of an effort to address retention issues stemming from the changing racial and ethnic composition of student populations (Padilla and Martinez, 2005). To a great extent, leadership for change reflected both social movement leadership and rational institutional responses to shifting academic characteristics and needs of students.

During the 1970s, with racial and ethnic minority group members becoming part of the faculty ranks, issues of mentoring for minority faculty members arose as concerns and, at some sites, as a support mechanism (Garcia, 2000; Lamb, 1999; Murrell, Crosby, and Ely, 1999). At the institutional level, minority faculty mentoring programs often became efforts to change minority faculty to avoid addressing and changing "the possible underlying tensions embedded in the organizational structure" (Smith, Smith, and Markham, 2000, p. 260). Although external pressures on higher education from minority communities waned during this period in comparison with the 1960s, activist students and faculty inside institutions of higher education pushed for organizational change. As a result, leadership for diversity during this period came mostly from activist faculty, graduate and undergraduate students, and staff who created support networks and programs on campuses to provide academic support services for minority students. These academic support services served to promote a sense of community that was different from but part of the larger campus community (Kramer and Weiner, 1994; Padilla and Martinez, 2005).

Perhaps the most contested issue in higher education regarding diversity during the 1970s was curriculum change. Although many white faculty members in higher education had supported civil rights issues during the 1960s, including providing access to minority college students, they were much less willing to change themselves and their campuses to accommodate the interests and concerns of minority students once they were on campus (Blauner, 1972). Similar to the rest of American society, white faculty underestimated the depth of change needed in American higher education to meet the visions promoted by leaders in the civil rights movement. White faculty assumed that changes taking place in society regarding social justice issues would eventually trickle into higher education. In a sense, institutions of higher education did not promote the efforts of white faculty to bring changes to their environment and culture such as the ones taking place in society.

In the 1980s, economic restructuring, a renewed emphasis on entrepreneurship, and the privatization of government services created a context of financial retrenchment pressures in higher education that affected minority programs. One result was the clustering of minority-specific curriculum programs such as Chicano studies and black studies under the rubric of ethnic studies (Aguirre, 2005). In this context of scarce resources, the ideology of reverse racism began to gain ascendance among white Americans across the United States. As white perceptions of reverse discrimination increased in higher education, diversity efforts felt the continuing backlash of the dominant group on both financial and cultural fronts. As reactionary pressures against affirmative action in higher education mounted across a broad range of public discourses and in the nation's highest courts, racial incidents on campuses across the country reinforced the perilous climate for diversity in higher education (Aguirre, 1994; Hudson, 1995; Sawires and Peacock, 2000; Winbush, 1999).

During the 1980s, the struggle for diversity in higher education focused on curriculum change, especially in the humanities and social sciences (LaBelle and Ward, 1996). Serious questions were raised as to what it meant to be an educated person in an emergent global society. The core curriculum of a liberal education and the Euro-American canon it represented came under sustained criticism, and the curriculum became the focal point of struggles for diversity in higher education, giving rise to cultural wars (Arthur and Shapiro, 1995; Padilla and Montiel, 1998). Although cultural relativism was recognized as an important aspect of human existence as early as the seventeenth century, cultural pluralism was not emphasized as an important value in American higher education until the campus wars of the 1980s. This emphasis was given impetus by the rise of epistemological postmodernism, which posed significant questions about, among other things, scientific methodology, power and the production of knowledge, the role of the subject in knowledge, and problems associated with representing knowledge through language (Mirchandani, 2005). Politically, the campus cultural wars over diversity took the form of "identity politics" or "politics of difference"—an ideological rejection of assimilation in favor of a view that reframed equality as the participation and inclusion of all groups, a view of equality that sometimes requires different treatment for oppressed or disadvantaged groups.

According to proponents of multicultural curriculum transformation, it is important to revise "eurocentric curriculum content to include the representation of those traditionally under- or unrepresented in it, as well as on innovating altogether new curricula that, from [their] inception, [are] already multiculturally inclusive" (Clark, 2002, p. 38). In some cases, proponents of multicultural curricular change received some financial support from foundations and philanthropic organizations to integrate racial and ethnic minorities in the curriculum (Institute for Higher Education Policy, 2004).

Not surprisingly, ardent supporters of the traditional curriculum and its Eurocentric foundations sounded the alarm about the multicultural threat and rose up in its defense. Perhaps the most eloquent of the defenders of the traditional canon was Bloom (1987), who noted that cultural relativism "succeeds in destroying the West's universal or intellectually imperialistic claims, leaving it to be just another culture. . . . Unfortunately the West is defined by its need for justification of its ways or values, by its need for discovery of nature, by its need for philosophy and science. This is its cultural imperative. Deprived of that, it will collapse" (p. 39). Fortunately, the transformation of the traditional curriculum did not lead to the demise of science, philosophy, or the academy. It has, however, broadened the learning experiences of students and their understanding of themselves and intergroup relations (Chang, Witt, Jones, and Hakuta, 2003; Gurin, Lehman, and Lewis, 2004).

Infusing multiculturalism into the curriculum tended to take two approaches: (1) implementing breadth requirements for students that provided courses focused on cultural pluralism, race relations, and diversity; and (2) revising existing areas of concentration and creating new ones in the humanities and social sciences focused on aspects of racial and ethnic minority group experiences and cultures. Stanford University, for example, changed the emphasis of a required class for freshmen students from Western culture to culture, ideas, and values. At Georgetown University, the English department created concentrations that broadened the study of literature in relation to social contexts, values, and institutions. Neither approach sought to eliminate the traditional canon from the curriculum. Rather, these approaches sought to expand the range of course offerings to include perspectives and experiences of racial and ethnic minority groups in society who were excluded from the curriculum.

Nevertheless, defenders of the traditional curriculum, many of whom were and are from outside the academy, misrepresented the changes as eliminating the Western canon. Indeed, scholars such as Sacks and Thiel (1995) framed curriculum changes at Stanford as portending the destruction of Western civilization on campuses. As the cultural wars spilled out into the larger society, defenders of the traditional canon used the media to publicly attack higher education institutions committed to multicultural curricular change. Working with organizations such as the American Council of Trustees and Alumni, the National Association of Scholars, and the Center for Equal Opportunity, the defenders of the traditional curriculum sought to mobilize the American public against diversity changes in higher education and against affirmative action in general. The National Association of Scholars, for instance, uses its Web page and its journal, *Academic Questions,* to promote its mission statement on diversity in higher education: "American higher education has been profoundly compromised in the past three decades. Standards have been eroded, the curriculum has been debased, and research has been trivialized or distorted by ideology" (www.nas.org). Overall, leadership for multicultural curriculum change in higher education reflects a broad mix of social movement struggles, institutional compromises, and routine policy changes. In the 1990s, the rational-bureaucratic approach to institutional change became more prominent as a strategy with the importation of leadership initiatives from the business sector.

Strategic planning in higher education leadership is a relatively recent phenomenon, although it was common in the private sector through the 1960s. It was not until the 1980s that higher education and the public sector began to use the mechanism of strategic planning (Morrill, 2000). Faced by changes in their environments, colleges and universities began to consider strategic planning as a way of confronting a future different from the present (Fuller, 1976; Kotler and Murphy, 1981). Initially used in the 1960s for facilities and space planning, strategic planning came to be used in the 1980s "as a rational tool for orderly, systematic advancement of the academic enterprise" (Dooris, Kelley, and Trainer, 2004, p. 6). Although different models of strategic planning have been developed (Fuller, 1976; Kotler and Murphy, 1981; Keller, 1983), most have several factors in common: environmental scanning, visioning and strategy formulation, strategy implementation, and evaluation and control (Trainer, 2004).

Starting at the end of the 1980s and moving into the 1990s, colleges and universities began to use strategic planning to address diversity issues (Hubbard, 1998). In some instances, diversity was an element of the overall strategic planning process, and in others diversity was the entire focus of the planning process. Although plagued by challenges in moving from formulation to implementation, strategic planning in higher education moved from the faddish application of linear formulaic approaches to challenging assumptions and emphasizing organizational learning. In this context, colleges and universities were expected to walk the talk rather than simply posturing in a normative environment that emphasized strategic planning activities that more often than not resulted in "shelf plans." Despite the emphasis on rational processes, strategic planning, especially diversity planning, became fraught with power plays and accommodations that reflected the interests of competing groups in higher education (for a discussion of how rationality promotes organizational control over members, see Eckstein, 1976). Strategic planning for diversity as a result faced many pressures and demands that blocked organizational responses to change (Bringle and Hatcher, 1996; Julius, Baldridge, and Pfeffer, 1999; Shapiro and Nunez, 2001).

Unsurprisingly, in an effort to confront campus pressures and demands opposing diversity planning processes in higher education, campus leaders such as presidents and chancellors spearheaded diversity initiatives. To transform higher education institutions, the diversity planning process sought to raise awareness about diversity issues on campus and to provide opportunities for minority groups to provide input in the development of programmatic activities for promoting diversity on campus. Perhaps one of the first efforts in higher education to link campus leadership with strategic planning for diversity was launched by faculty members at the University of Colorado System in 1986.

In 1987, minority faculty at the University of Colorado System provided a critique of the institution's strategic planning activities in relation to ethnic minorities and provided a set of recommendations to improve relations between the university and minority communities. The report, *Minorities and Strategic Planning at the University of Colorado,* called on the university to develop the capacity to transform itself into a multicultural institution by integrating minority issues in its strategic planning processes and initiatives. Since then the University of Colorado System has developed several diversity plans, and its campuses have done the same. In 1991, in her inaugural address, President Judith Albino called on the university community to commit to the "imperative of diversity." In the 1990s, each of the university's campuses developed and implemented diversity plans. In 1999, the board of regents issued a statement reaffirming the university's commitment to diversity by providing a set of principles for developing campus diversity plans that, among other things, rejected quotas and set-asides and promoted the use of race- and ethnicity-neutral approaches where "promising." In 2002, the Diversity Task Force of CU Vision 2010 submitted a report to the president calling for a vision of the university that promotes constructive engagement across lines of difference.

In 1988, the University of Wisconsin System adopted a long-range plan to promote diversity across the state's twenty-six institutions of higher education. *Design for Diversity* was a ten-year plan based on the view that a public university should serve all the people of a state, including race and ethnic minorities. In 1993, the University of Wisconsin System conducted a midpoint review of the plan's progress, recommitting itself to many of the original activities, modifying others, and discontinuing still others. In 1998, the plan was renewed for another ten years as *Plan 2008: Educational Quality Through Racial and Ethnic Diversity. Plan 2008* continues to shape diversity efforts in Wisconsin's institutions of higher education. In its *Diversity Report* in 2004, the University of Wisconsin System acknowledged the importance of going beyond managing racial and ethnic diversity to a broader understanding of diversity that includes difference. This recognition may give rise to a diversity initiative that may truly seek to transform the institutions of higher education in Wisconsin.

By the end of the 1990s, diversity planning had become yet another trend in higher education, with many institutions using the mechanism as a means for addressing issues of underrepresentation and exclusion. Its effectiveness, however, has been limited. A common complaint among diversity proponents is that diversity initiatives were not integrated into the core structures of their respective colleges and universities (Humphreys, 2000). Moreover, white faculty were often unwilling to contribute to the promotion of diversity on campus (Brayboy, 2003; Lowe, 1999). Although faculty in general may perceive higher education as committed to diversity, few actually go out of their way to promote diversity (Aguirre, 2000). Instead, they may covertly resist diversity by accepting only a few minority members in their departments and programs. For example, although it may be illegal to use quotas to promote diversity, white faculty use "informal quotas" to limit the presence of minorities and women faculty to one or two members of academic units (Chesler, Lewis, and Crowfoot, 2005).

Although strategic planning processes for diversity may have considerable potential for contributing to the transformation of colleges and universities, one can observe by examining the cases in Colorado and Wisconsin that the idea of becoming diverse organizations is not clearly embedded in their efforts, which continue to emphasize representation rather than transformation. The challenge for leadership in higher education is for it to go beyond the notion of presenting or showcasing minorities to that of creating inclusive organizations that hold diversity as a core value and embody it in their operations and institutional practices. For instance, minority-serving institutions, where one might expect to find diverse organizational features, are not much different from predominantly white institutions in terms of culture: both sets of institutions reflect the values and practices of the dominant group in society (Bridges, Holmes, Morelon, and Williams, 2004).

Summary

We noted in the preceding two chapters that diversity occupies a precarious position in American higher education. This situation poses a serious dilemma for higher education because an abundance of evidence is available, whether based on research or casual observation, to show that American society is becoming more diverse. The dilemma for higher education increases in importance if higher education is unable to reframe itself to provide leadership and leaders for an increasingly diverse society. Not only is globalization bringing the world closer together; American society in the twenty-first century will require people to demonstrate the social and human capital necessary for forming meaningful and respectful social relations in a highly diverse environment. Institutions of higher education in the twenty-first century will be challenged in their response to diversity as a social force with the potential for changing institutional structures and arrangements. As the United States assumes a larger and more prominent role in the global economy, it becomes imperative that institutions of higher education develop organizational cultures and environments that respond effectively to issues and concerns about diversity.

In an effort to understand how institutions of higher education have responded to diversity issues and concerns, this chapter examined two types of organizational strategies, co-optation and transformation, they have used to frame their leadership responses to focus on diversity. Our discussion and comparison of how higher education and economic organizations frame leadership responses to diversity was intended to illustrate how the synergistic relationship between diversity and organizational culture is defined by an organization's conceptualization of diversity. That is, we sought to illustrate how an organization's definition of diversity can result in leaders' responses that might not be replicated across different types of organizations, such as higher education versus business organizations. To this end, we conceptualized transformational organizational strategies as those that conceive of diversity as a social force, whereas co-optation organizational strategies treat diversity as a descriptive dimension. In higher education organizations, the former seek to use diversity as an agent of change in the organizational culture, while in business organizations, the latter seek to use diversity to create superficial images for its presence in the organizational culture. We noted in this chapter that the problem for higher education is that it has attempted to avoid challenging its organizational culture by borrowing leadership practices from business organizations that treat diversity as a representative and descriptive feature.

We also discussed in this chapter how organizational leadership strategies focused on diversity in higher education are responses to social and demographic changes in society—especially the need for institutions of higher education to adapt to increasing racial and ethnic diversity and emergent multiculturalism in American society. We suggested in this chapter that leadership strategies in higher education that are capable of transforming organizational culture have the most promise for changing higher education to be more inclusive of diversity. Transformational organizational strategies also enhance the context for leadership practices that lead for diversity in higher education. In contrast, co-optation organizational strategies that treat diversity as a descriptive measure result in leadership practices that are selective in their responses to diversity, practices that seek only to incorporate diversity as organizational practice in higher education. When treated as a descriptive dimension, leadership practices in higher education are diverse only to the extent that they benefit an organization's pursuit of goals (co-optation).

Finally, from a broader social perspective, transforming colleges and universities into diverse organizations is hampered by the nature of structured inequalities that favor the dominant white group, in some cases including white women over racial and ethnic minority groups. The emergence of "culture wars" on college and university campuses in the United States, for example, illustrated the importance of understanding the relative difference in power relations between the dominant group and minority groups, especially regarding knowledge production. Diversity cannot survive if it is portrayed as a threat to institutional integrity and diversity leadership is treated as an unwelcome participant in the organizational culture of higher education. As we observed in this chapter, as institutions of higher education seek to move from using co-optation strategies to diversity planning approaches that are transformational, they must adopt more comprehensive models of organizational change. Because comprehensive changes are embedded in struggles over institutional legitimacy between the dominant group and minority groups, however, resistance to change limits the realization of strategic changes. Moreover, even if struggles between the dominant group and minority groups were absent in higher education, it would be extremely difficult to bring about strategic changes because of the many challenges inherent in managing communications, employee morale and commitment, and the change initiatives themselves. Intergroup struggles between the dominant group and minority groups exacerbate all these challenges and slow, if not stop, progress in promoting diversity in higher education.

Practicing Diversity Leadership in Higher Education

SINCE JUSTICE POWELL'S OPINION IN *BAKKE* regarding the use of a "diversity rationale" in higher education admissions to enhance the complexion of student populations, it has become increasingly difficult to talk about diversity in higher education. Despite the decisions in *Grutter, Gratz,* and *Hopwood* that diversity is a compelling interest for institutions of higher education, diversity initiatives continue to face tough challenges in higher education (Aguirre and Martinez, 2003a). We showed in the first chapter that the American public and primary stakeholders in higher education perceive diversity issues and concerns as important and vital in higher education's mission to prepare students for living and working in a diverse society. In the second chapter, we argued that diversity is an important factor in shaping perceptions in higher education about effective leadership practices. And in the preceding chapter, we illustrated the use of competing organizational practices in higher education leadership that either promote diversity as necessary for organizational change or use diversity as a tool for stabilizing organizations or avoiding destabilization in a changing environment.

This chapter uses the conceptual framework for organizational strategies focused on diversity leadership developed in the previous chapter to discuss the effect of diversity leadership on the organizational culture and institutional climate in higher education, especially its effect in target areas such as student recruitment, curriculum reform, academic support, faculty recruitment, administrator recruitment, and institutional mission and vision (Hurtado, Milem, Clayton-Pedersen, and Allen, 1999; Kezar, 2001; Smith, Turner, Osei-Kofi, and Richards, 2004). The previous chapter distinguished between rational-bureaucratic approaches that co-opt and manage diversity and transformative approaches that lead for diversity by transforming exclusive institutions of higher education into inclusive ones. Leadership practices in higher education that manage diversity treat diversity as a problem, whereas practices that lead for diversity treat diversity as an opportunity for changing organizations. For example, "managing diversity" prevents human resource–related crises in an organization; that is, diversity is treated as a tool for developing contingency strategies with a changing environment (Davidson, 1999; Hu-Dehart, 2000). In contrast, treating diversity as a social force creates the opportunity for change in organizations; that is, diversity is treated as a vehicle for bringing organizations into congruity with a changing environment (Bass, 1999; Gregory, 1996).

The discussion in this chapter is a synthesis of the issues discussed in the previous chapters. More important, the discussion in the previous chapters has provided the language, concepts, and issues integral to a discussion in this chapter of how diversity leadership is practiced in higher education. The synthesis will enhance our understanding of diversity leadership and the components associated with it. It will assist us in identifying factors or components in the organizational culture in higher education that create the capacity for practicing diversity leadership. The synthesis will allow us to observe how practicing diversity leadership is necessary for the promotion of culturally proficient institutions of higher education. To illustrate the challenges faced by diversity leadership in higher education, we offer some observations in this chapter regarding the dilemmas faced by minority administrators and practitioners. Two questions guide the discussion in this chapter:

Why is practicing diversity leadership necessary for building inclusive institutions of higher education?

What is the organizational nexus for diversity leadership and culturally proficient institutions of higher education?

Higher Education's Response to Diversity Initiatives

The organizational co-optation of diversity and leadership practices in higher education has been used as strategy for changing organizations in the twenty-first century. Given the demographic shifts swirling around institutions of higher education, the use of co-optation strategies has sought to create a more adaptive organizational culture and institutional climate in higher education. The attempts to make higher education institutions more adaptive to diversity, however, have had unfavorable outcomes for diversity itself. In particular, they have resulted in competing definitions of diversity in higher education. For example, Bunzel (2001) notes that the word "'diversity' has been used in so many different ways it now means whatever one wants it to mean. . . . The elasticity of the [word] 'diversity' has masked many kinds of questionable conduct" (pp. 494–495).

Some types of questionable conduct associated with higher education's use of the word *diversity* are window-dressing approaches that aim to co-opt diversity to create an artificial image that welcomes racial and ethnic minorities to the institution, diversity training programs that aim to alter individual's biases but not organizational biases against minorities, curricular changes that use racial and ethnic minorities as subjects for study but not as contributors to the knowledge base in academia, and diversity recruitment efforts that do not change the dominant group's perception that minorities are academic inferiors who are pushing their way into higher education at the expense of dominant group members (Bernard, 2005; Bollag, 2005; Munoz, Jasis, Young, and McLaren, 2004; Williams, Nakashima, Kich, and Reginald, 1996).

Depending on the location of a particular institution in the highly stratified system of higher education in the United States, the use of institutional approaches for focusing on diversity varies across students, faculty, staff, administrators, curricula, institutional culture and values, and informal relations among other organizational dimensions. For example, at community colleges one finds relatively higher concentrations of racial and ethnic minority students than at four-year institutions of higher education (Gutierrez, Castaneda, and Katsinas, 2002). Despite the high concentration of racial and ethnic minority students, however, the organizational culture of community colleges continues to reflect the values and interests of the dominant group instead of reflecting diversity and multicultural changes in their environments such as the recruitment and retention of minority faculty and administrators and minorities (Bower, 2002; Pope, 2002). In contrast, in highly selective and exclusive institutions of higher education such as Ivy League institutions, one finds fewer minorities altogether but greater use of co-optation strategies—from students to administrators to "minority programs" that are added to the institutions' core programs (Arenson, 2005; Graduate Employees and Student Organizations, 2005; Roach, 1999; Thomas, 1994).

During the 1990s, diversity training became one of the fastest-growing industries in the country and contributed to changes in the organizational features of higher education. Indeed, elements of diversity training became commodified, with access to resources and materials that once were shared freely in the public domain (via the Internet, for example) becoming restricted to those willing to pay for them. Diversity consultants emerged to provide presentations, seminars, and workshops on managing diversity to corporations, colleges, and universities across the country willing to pay for such services (Armour, 2003; Fisher, 2004; Hyter, 2004). In a sense, the organizational response to diversity was constructed as a scientific process with empirical validity as the "new" tool for verifying the presence of diversity in higher education. For institutions of higher education, diversity consultants became philosopher-kings who provided guidance to institutions of higher education on how to find an "expert diversity professional." Whether or not diversity consultants and diversity workshops contributed to improvements on college and university campuses cannot be readily discerned and remains a topic for badly needed research. As with other politically sensitive issues in higher education, diversity consultants at least made it appear that something was being done to bring about organizational change.

The efforts of diversity consultants and diversity workshops, however, often had limited outcomes in higher education because of the constant changes among those who occupy senior leadership positions in colleges and universities; diversity efforts, like many other efforts, tended to end with the tenure of those who launched them (Corrigan, 1995). Unfortunately, most persons in senior leadership positions seek to leave their personal imprint on their institution, usually as a means of getting a more senior position or moving on to a higher-status institution. Persons seeking to move into or out of senior leadership positions in higher education often distance themselves from the work or achievements of their predecessors to highlight their own work, even if it means abandoning institutional initiatives launched by efforts of the latter group. As such, a serious challenge to diversity leadership in higher education is a lack of continuity in promoting diversity initiatives by senior leadership in higher education (Williams, 2005; Yates, 2002).

Management, Leadership, and Diversity

It is relatively well known that a substantive difference exists between managing and leading an organization, and although the distinction between the two is neither hard nor fast and some overlap occurs, the two activities are not interchangeable. Managing constitutes the rational day-to-day control and problem-solving activities that go on in an organization. That is, managing involves influencing people to perform tasks that are tied to personal ideas of how things should be done in the organization. Leading, on the other hand, provides vision for the organization and motivates people to achieve major organizational goal changes. That is, leading requires that leaders change themselves to motivate others to change to transform the organization. One could argue that the chief difference between managing and leading is focus: managing uses power and privilege to get people to subscribe to organizational expectations regarding performance, whereas leading promotes change as a vehicle for organizational members to transform organizations as a collective enterprise.

Relative to diversity, leadership today is most frequently defined in terms of change leadership or transformational leadership. Management, on the other hand, is more often associated with co-optation activities. The two approaches overlap sufficiently so that some diversity initiatives in higher education can be seen as falling within both approaches, and some scholars emphasize a change orientation in management frameworks by writing about managing change and managing diversity—perhaps a point between the two approaches. Management and leadership can be related to co-optation and transformation approaches to produce four types of management and leadership strategies: (1) bureaucratic management, (2) reactive leadership, (3) change-oriented management, and (4) transformational leadership (see Exhibit 4). (We discussed bureaucratic management, change-oriented management, and transformational leadership in the previous chapter.) Reactive leadership, in relation

EXHIBIT 4
Organizational Management and Leadership Approaches

	Management	Leadership
Co-optation	Bureaucratic Management	Reactive Leadership
Transformational	Change-Oriented Management	Transformational Leadership

to diversity, is leadership that seeks to bring about organizational or environmental changes to protect the privileged status of the dominant group. It goes beyond bureaucratic management by emphasizing a broad-based vision about a color-blind social order without addressing the historical structures that limit the rise of such an order. As such, it is a feature of contemporary society that must be contended with by those seeking to promote diversity in higher education.

The nesting of reactive leadership in the ideology of color-blindness is highly appealing to the public in general, but it is also appealing to higher education institutions that do not connect the structural features of society from the past to those of the present and the future (Brown and others, 2003; Killian, 1990). Wallace (2003) has noted that "we are still not a color blind society, integration has not been achieved, and the 'dream' of Dr. King has not been realized. Equal opportunity and race neutral concepts have not been achieved because many refuse to recognize the past, and assume that simply declaring equality, integration and a color blind society will magically make it happen" (p. 707).

In other words, color-blindness offers a vision, much like the great African American leader Martin Luther King, Jr., did in the 1960s, where members of society are judged by the content of their character rather than by the color of their skin. Although Martin Luther King, Jr., envisioned a color-blind society, he did not and probably could not tell us how to get there (Berry, 1996; Bonilla-Silva, 2003a; Steinhorn and Diggs-Brown, 1999). Getting there is more difficult than simply envisioning a color-blind society. Individual attitudes and behaviors, institutional racism, reactionary movements by the dominant group, and economic, political, and cultural dynamics make it exceptionally difficult to get there (Bonilla-Silva, 2003b; Brown and others, 2003; Killian, 1990; Turner, 1996). For example, the Education Department's Office of Civil Rights under the current Bush Administration discourages colleges and universities from using race-conscious policies despite the series of court rulings that affirm their legality and instead promotes the use of race-neutral approaches.

In some cases, color-blindness appeals to racial and ethnic minorities because it offers a vision of a society where they will no longer be judged by the color of their skin but by the merits of their accomplishments. Dillard (2004) argues, however, that minorities are recruited by the conservative right to promote the creation of a color-blind society that undermines civil rights for minorities. In general, a color-blind perspective is an ideal vision: it jumps over many societal phases and stages where the dominant group overcomes its racial and other biases and accepts members of other ethnic groups as equals and then begins to systematically dismantle the social structures that favor dominant group members. Movement toward a color-blind society involves inclusion of the views, perspectives, and interests of other groups in addressing institutional and societal problems, especially in framing the problems and their solutions.

Currently, color-blindness involves forced assimilation of "others" in Euro-American society. It does not value cultural pluralism or diversity and refuses to recognize the persisting racial dynamics that characterize the United States today. According to Bonilla-Silva, Lewis, and Embrick (2004), racial stories told by members of the dominant group that accompany color-blind racism reinforce rather than contest racial inequality in U.S. society. Indeed, color-blind racism is part of a reactionary movement led by the dominant group that seeks to diminish the value of diversity to society to protect Euro-American privileges. The aim of color-blind racism is to mold diversity into monocultural Americanism as a means of ensuring that the dominant group's perspectives of democracy and social justice prevail into the future (Aguirre, 2004). In this context, diversity leadership in higher education becomes all the more necessary for building inclusive institutions of higher education that can maintain a diverse pipeline of professionals and intellectuals who are able to recognize the value and importance of diversity for themselves and who can provide the leadership necessary to break down the exclusive barriers that the dominant group has constructed to ensure its privileged position in society.

Diversity Readiness and Awareness

Both co-optation and transformation approaches to diversity in higher education emphasize diversity awareness activities intended to increase understanding on campuses relative to diversity (Sutton, 1998; Tatum, 2000). Such diversity awareness activities provide opportunities for participants in higher education institutions to understand the nature and forms of group domination and oppression in society and to examine themselves in relation to those dynamics (Heller, 1989; Springer, 1996). Indeed, changes in individual attitudes and behaviors toward diversity often are promoted through self-reflexive small groups that cause individuals to examine their own biases relative to minority groups (Lewis, Chesler, and Forman, 2000; Morrow, Burris-Kitchen, and Der-Karabetian, 2000; Solorzano, Ceja, and Yosso, 2000). The challenge for diversity leadership in higher education is to construct and promote practices and strategies that change biases or prejudices toward racial and ethnic minorities as part of a long-term approach to change in organizational culture and climate.

For example, Colorado State University at Pueblo (CSU–Pueblo), a regional public institution, is in a community where the American and Spanish Mexican cultures met and collided in the early and middle parts of the nineteenth century. In the early part of the twentieth century, the city was a company town for the Rockefeller family and its economic empire. The city's culture and racial dynamics reflect the historical struggles between the dominant and minority groups, with Anglo Americans and assimilated Italian Americans maintaining privileged positions in the community and Mexicans struggling to assume political power and entrepreneurial integration. In short, the environment surrounding CSU–Pueblo was shaped by an unstable climate for diversity.

In spring 2005, a Mexican American freshman female student accused a tenured senior anthropology professor at CSU–Pueblo of making derogatory remarks about Mexicans during a class session in which he allegedly ranted and raved about illegal Mexican immigrants, yelling and pounding a book on the desk, using profanity, and saying "screw you" when the complaining student walked out of the session. An investigation by the campus administration documented the view of other students in the class that the comments could have been perceived as offensive to Hispanics. The official campus investigation concluded that it could not find sufficient evidence of racially oriented statements or derogatory comments against the complaining student. But the investigation did find that the professor's teaching style and conduct in the classroom could lead some students to continued perceptions of a racially hostile classroom and institutional climate.

In an attempt to alleviate perceptions in the community that the university maintained a racially hostile climate and to educate the campus community about diversity, university officials sponsored a series of open forums on campus promoting increased respect for diversity. The open forums made it obvious that the university lacked the necessary infrastructure to promote an effective campaign for diversity on campus. Although CSU–Pueblo became a Hispanic-serving institution at the turn of the decade, it lacked a campus climate supportive of diversity and noticeable numbers of Hispanics in faculty and administrative positions, especially at the senior level. Moreover, despite the fact that it had developed institutional diversity plans over the years, they had been shelved and never implemented as part of an organizational strategy intended to transform the institution into an inclusive organization. The result was that the open forums on campus designed to promote respect and tolerance for diversity served to present a public stance against racism but did not result in a campuswide diversity initiative that challenged resistance to change in the institution's culture and climate.

Although organizational strategies to promote diversity such as the open forums at CSU–Pueblo may serve to cool off individuals offended by incidents on campus, they seldom lead to full-blown initiatives to incorporate diversity as a core value of an institution—which is not to say that the use of open forums is not helpful in promoting diversity on campus. They certainly can be, especially when they are part of a multilevel strategy that seeks not only to increase awareness of exclusionary practices and biases that target diversity but also to motivate individuals to cooperate in overcoming them. Open forums can be used in tandem with other organizational practices to meet specific goals for diversity. For example, when two fraternities at Auburn University dressed in black face for Halloween, it created a perception on campus and in the community that diversity was unwelcome on campus. The campus administration responded to the incident by sponsoring public forums and workshops on diversity and formed a diversity leadership council (Yates, 2002). The purpose of the council was to develop a comprehensive blueprint for promoting and implementing diversity initiatives on campus. As such, the incident served as an opportunity for integrating diversity as a core value in the institution.

Leadership in higher education must be cautious about not allowing the use of organizational activities such as open forums about diversity to result in a perception that the institution seeks to manage diversity by focusing on co-opting representative aspects of diversity rather than using diversity for institutional transformation. For example, leadership in higher education often uses open forums to manage the representational aspects of diversity by focusing on the enrollment of students from underrepresented groups. But although the focus is on increasing the enrollment of underrepresented groups, leadership in higher education does not address principal issues that manage their enrollment such as providing financial aid and scholarship support that would result in a more robust pipeline for underrepresented students (McMillen, 1990; Rendon and Hope, 1996). Simply increasing the number of underrepresented students will not change how a higher education institution's culture and climate respond to diversity. To avoid the perception that a higher education institution is managing diversity through the enrollment of underrepresented students, leadership in higher education must also change alienating and hostile institutional climates such as the ones described at CSU–Pueblo and Auburn that diminish learning opportunities for underrepresented students (Sullivan, Esmail, and Soh, 2002). The challenge for institutions of higher education, especially in the twenty-first century, is to use leadership practices to transform themselves into truly inclusive learning environments where students of color feel that their views are represented and respected in the organizational culture and climate. Only diversity leadership can provide the vision and the energy required to transform institutions of higher education.

Leaders in higher education need to undergo the same personal transformational changes that students and faculty are expected to undergo as they pursue diversity initiatives on campus (Brown, 1998). It is not enough for leaders—presidents, provosts, deans, and other administrators—to pay lip service to diversity. Leaders in higher education must not only endorse diversity as a core value in the institutions they serve but also understand the social dynamics of domination and oppression and their effects on diversity. If leaders are unable or unwilling to transform themselves to be change agents for diversity, they cannot provide the leadership necessary for building diverse and inclusive institutions of higher education. Their leadership efforts will remain at the level of managing diversity.

Developing Capacity for Diversity Leadership

The development of leadership in higher education with the capacity to effectively address diversity issues and concerns remains a major challenge (Chahin, 1993; Chesler, Lewis, and Crowfoot, 2005; Hale, 2004). Despite the work of several higher education organizations such as the American Association of University Professors and the American Council on Education diversity is generally relegated to the margins of many leadership development programs. The centering of higher education leadership practices in a Eurocentric consciousness continues to challenge the use of the diversity paradigm to change the social context for higher education and society (Dowdy, 1998; Wagner, 2005). A result from practicing leadership centered in a Eurocentric consciousness has been the persistence of a managerial approach to diversity in higher education that treats diversity as a representational dimension in the organizational culture and climate—a guise for protecting dominant group interests.

One reason that higher education has been unable to uncouple leadership from its Eurocentric roots is that institutions of higher education do not prepare leaders of higher education to deal with emerging challenges to organizational culture and climate. An organizational conundrum exists regarding leadership in higher education because people usually pursue leadership roles through their own initiative rather than as a response to social justice concerns in society (Birnbaum, 1988; Green, 1988). In addition, people perceive leadership roles in higher education as a task-oriented activity rather than as an opportunity with the potential to bring about organizational change (Diamond, 2002; Hill, Green, and Eckel, 2001; Hubbard, 1998; Nelsen, 1994). If leadership in higher education is treated as a task-oriented activity, then diversity becomes a challenge to leadership because leadership itself will be unable to use the potential diversity offers for transforming organizations. As a result, leadership for diversity is missing from institutions of higher education because leaders do not incorporate diversity in their leadership endeavors and activities (Ewell, 1985; Mitchell and Kumar, 2001; O'Donnell and Green-Merritt, 1997). As noted in the first chapter, the American public considers diversity education important and necessary for building leadership capacity in higher education.

Developing the capacity for diversity leadership in higher education is only now beginning to gain some scholarly attention. Institutions of higher education have not ignored the need for diversity leadership. Instead, they have been misguided in their incorporation of models from business organizations for dealing with diversity that have resulted in management approaches to diversity that are not compatible in an environment sensitive to knowledge production as a tool for social change. The emphasis on managing diversity in higher education failed to acknowledge the importance of *diverse leadership* comprising racial and ethnic diversity and *leadership diversity* as a rubric for addressing diversity. Consequently, institutions of higher education recognized the presence of diversity issues and concerns but did not incorporate diversity leadership in the organizational culture as a vehicle for redressing diversity issues and concerns.

To develop the capacity for leadership focused on diversity, leaders in higher education, including diverse leadership, must be provided with diversity leadership development opportunities for them to position themselves in relation to the nature of the challenge for promoting diversity in higher education (Farmer, 1997; Hrabowski, 2004; Phillips and Blumberg, 1982). In particular, understanding the challenges faced by diverse leadership is important for its own experiences and for navigating the sea of issues it faces in higher education (Castenell and Tarule, 1997). Unfortunately, most leadership development programs continue to address the pipeline issue and to focus on preparing those interested in assuming administrative roles. Higher education needs the emergence of diverse leadership, leadership with a deep understanding of the challenges it faces in transforming institutions of higher education.

The Dilemma of Diverse Leadership

Diverse leadership faces several dilemmas in the public arena. Martinez (2005) has adapted the dilemmas to make them more applicable to diverse leadership in higher education:

Role expectations for diverse leadership in higher education do not coincide with its own perceptions, goals, or expectations regarding diversity.

Unresponsive institutional policies put diversity leadership in marginalized positions vis-à-vis the institution and the campus communities it represents.

Diverse leadership is put in a buffer position between the higher education institution and minority communities, thereby constraining diversity leadership's ability to make meaningful decisions but being expected to assume the responsibilities for programmatic failures and "cooling out" community frustrations.

Professional advancement in the higher education institution is generally a result of adherence to its normative environment; as such, diverse leadership is expected to demonstrate its institutional value by implementing co-optation practices with minority communities.

Institutions of higher education continue to limit the institutional capacity for diverse leadership to service delivery and communications with minority group members.

Diverse communities in higher education often expect more from diverse leadership in higher education than it can deliver.

Institutions of higher education seek to promote "super" but safe diverse leadership, often to display it as a showpiece.

The dilemmas experienced by diverse leadership in higher education are embedded in a normative order that emphasizes compliance with the values of the dominant group and the constraints associated with the position it occupies in the organizational structure (Herbert, 1974; Tien, 1998). In an ideal diverse organization where leaders are proficient in promoting practices that promote diversity, the dilemmas would not exist. Nevertheless, until inclusive and diverse organizations are developed, these dilemmas will continue to haunt diverse leaders in higher education.

Practicing Diversity Leadership

The practice of diversity leadership in higher education requires experienced leaders and administrators capable of understanding and embracing diversity. Development programs for these leaders must not only disseminate empirical knowledge about the perilous climate for diversity in society and higher education but also understand the tendency of higher education organizations to marginalize diversity as a value and to emphasize the core values of efficiency and effectiveness. Based on our discussion in this monograph, we offer the following observations for the practice of diversity leadership in higher education.

Proficient diversity leadership requires that leaders be able to transform themselves by making diversity a core value in their personal lives and in the organizational practices they promote. In transforming themselves, diverse leaders can challenge the dominant discourse that marginalizes diversity in higher education, making it powerless as a social force and change agent in society and higher education. Integral to proficient diversity leadership is the recognition that "leaders need to understand the ways they have constituted their own worlds, and realize that heightened consciousness of their position, beliefs, and role can lead to changes in those worlds" (Taylor, 1995, p. 66).

Proficient diversity leadership uses reference groups in higher education institutions to engage dominant and minority group members in collaborative strategies for promoting a democratic environment for diversity. As such, proficient diversity leadership promotes intergroup relations that reduce perceptions promoting negative images of diversity. Proficient diversity leaders must not only "understand how organizational groups and identity groups relate to each other" but also "look beyond leaders and followers to social, racial, and cultural issues that are outside organizational boundaries" (Mabokela and Madsen, 2003, p. 152).

Proficient diversity leadership must implement practices in the organizational culture of higher education that promote cultural competence as a vehicle for building multicultural institutions. Martin (1982) argues that even traditional leadership in higher education can be strengthened by building diversity and multiculturalism into the core character of higher education institutions. As a result, proficient diversity leadership uses cultural competency to promote multiculturalism as necessary for institutional change, leading institutional change to incorporate diversity into a community that values inquiry and reflection as tools for defining organizational mission and function.

In sum, proficient diversity leadership exhibits several characteristics (Alire, 2001; Jackson, 2006; Lopez-Mulnix and Mulnix, 2006; Mabokela and Madsen, 2003; Santiago, 1996; Sinclair, 2002, 2004; Taylor, 1995):

Promoting personal awareness and recognition of cultural and social differences in leadership practices;

Promoting leadership practices that encourage diversity as a challenge to traditional, static organizational structures;

Developing leadership capacity in organizational members (staff, students, and faculty) who work effectively with diversity;

Identifying and exploring the use of leadership strategies to challenge the obstacles faced by diversity in the organizational culture and climate;

Incorporating innovation in leadership practices that transform traditional leadership styles into ones that bring diversity from the periphery to the core of the institution's mission.

Cultural Proficiency and Practicing Diversity Leadership

Practicing diversity leadership is necessary for building a cultural proficiency model that includes diversity in higher education. A cultural proficiency model refers to the development of policies and practices that prepare institutions of higher education to interact effectively with a diverse racial and ethnic environment (Lindsey, Robins, and Terrell, 1999). Practicing diversity leadership increases the likelihood that organizational culture will be aligned with diversity issues and concerns in the higher education community. That is, practicing diversity leadership results in a closer fit between diversity and organizational effectiveness. For example, Ketchen and others (1997) have shown that organizations aligned with their environment perform better than organizations not aligned with their environment (see also Kozlowski and Doherty, 1989). Accordingly, effective leadership is associated with the capacity to construct and promote organizational practices that are a close fit between organization and environment, allowing for a higher level of cooperation, greater accessibility and exchange of information, and increased capacity to achieve organizational goals. As such, proficient diversity leadership would result in a higher level of cooperation between organizational culture and a diverse environment, especially resulting in greater accessibility (recruitment of diverse leaders, for example) and exchange of information (preparing students to function in a diverse society and workplace, for example).

If organizational alignment with the environment increases an organization's performance, then diversity leadership in higher education increases its chances of constructing effective organizational practices for a diverse environment, including primary stakeholders (faculty, students, and administrators) in higher education. Effective organizational practices are those perceived by participants in a diverse environment as leading for diversity because they implement diversity as a requirement for organizational success. As such, diversity leadership practices are not a corrective measure for institutional practices. Instead, diversity leadership is a tool for strengthening institutional practices that position diversity at the core of an institution's culture. A culturally responsive organization would thus reflect diversity as a principal component in its leadership. One manner in which institutions of higher education have responded to the need to lead for diversity is by increasing diversity among administrators and faculty (Aguirre and Martinez, 2002). Leading for diversity in higher education recognizes the need for developing cultural proficiency by incorporating multiculturalism in the curriculum and by diversifying the ranks of faculty and administrators (Andrews and Cavan, 2002; McNulty, 1995; Terenzini, Cabrera, and Colbeck, 2001; Vaughan, 1996; Winston, 2001). In other words, one goal is for higher education institutions to align themselves with an environment that is becoming increasingly diverse.

Implicit in the observation that organizations aligned with the environment perform better is the assumption that aligned organizations initiate actions that fuel a synergistic relationship between organization and environment. That is, aligned organizations initiate actions that increase the level of understanding and cooperation between organization and environment. As a result, the synergistic relationship between organization and environment enables participants to communicate freely between each other so that they can adapt to changes taking place in each other. For example, the use of leadership practices that are static and nonresponsive to changes in the environment is identified as an obstacle to making organizational culture more responsive to diversity (Behar-Horenstein and Amatea, 1996; Kezar, 2002). In addition, the portrayal of diversity as a problem constrains the treatment of diversity as a desirable feature in organizational culture.

Thus, leadership practices that are aligned with a diverse environment are more likely to result in an organizational culture that promotes difference among organizational participants as necessary for building a learning organization based on sharing and trust. For example, aligning leadership practices in higher education with a diverse environment has a positive influence on multiple forms of engagement by participants, especially diversity in engagement that is crucial to maintaining continuity in organizational culture (Johnston, 1996). Aligning leadership practices in higher education with a diverse environment also challenges the constraints imposed by sameness on organizational culture by promoting difference as a vehicle for creating higher education institutions that represent inclusive learning communities (Walker and Quong, 1998). Aligning leadership practices with diversity in higher education creates a mind-set in students and faculty that uses difference as a tool for critiquing existing knowledge and creating new meanings (Beane, 1998). In general, then, aligning leadership practices with a diverse environment increases the chances that higher education institutions will be culturally proficient because difference will be a positive influence in creating engagement in a learning community based on democratic ideals.

Summary

We began our discussion of diversity by examining public and stakeholders' perceptions of diversity in American higher education. A casual observation of one's community or reading the newspaper shows that American society is becoming more diverse. And as American society becomes more diverse, so will the social institutions that are vital to shaping a person's path through life. Indeed, the nation's future economic well-being will increasingly depend on the racial and ethnic minority groups that have been excluded from full participation in society. Consequently, it is becoming increasingly clear that U.S. society in the twenty-first century will require people to demonstrate the social and human capital necessary for forming meaningful and respectful social relations in a highly diverse environment. The responsibility for ensuring that individuals acquire the social and human capital required for living in a diverse society lies with the nation's educational systems, especially higher education.

As we argued in the previous chapter, higher education organizations in the twenty-first century will be challenged in their response to diversity as a social force or a descriptive dimension in society. If American social and economic organizations are to assume a larger role in tomorrow's global economy, higher education will have to develop the organizational cultures and environments that respond effectively to diversity in this country.

In this chapter we discussed the organizational response to diversity to illustrate the synergistic relationship between diversity and leadership practices in higher education. We argued that the manner by which institutions of higher education treat diversity will determine whether they will be inclusive of diversity or simply represent diversity in the organizational culture. We also argued that the demographic changes taking place in U.S. society challenge institutions of higher education to develop diversity strategies that are inclusive of racial and ethnic diversity in society. As a result, inclusive organizational strategies promote leadership practices that lead for diversity because they change organizational culture by reframing diversity as an inclusive process in a learning organization.

In contrast, representational organizational strategies promote leadership practices that are selective in their response to diversity and that seek only to incorporate diversity as organizational practice. These leadership practices transpose diversity as a wrinkle rather than an integrated process in the organizational culture. These leadership practices are diverse only to the extent that they benefit the higher education organization's pursuit of goals. For institutions of higher education to be more inclusive of racial and ethnic diversity in U.S. society, the next phase of higher education leadership requires diversity leadership that is transformational for both higher education and society.

References

Agathangelou, A., and Zalewski, M. (2005). Disturbing hegemony? *International Feminist Journal of Politics, 7,* 308–317.

Aguirre, A., Jr. (1994). *Racism in higher education: A perilous climate for minorities* (IHELG Monograph 93–8). Houston: Institute for Higher Education Law and Governance, University of Houston.

Aguirre, A., Jr. (2000). *Women and minority faculty in the academic workplace: Recruitment, retention, and academic culture.* ASHE-ERIC Higher Education Report, Vol. 27, No. 6. San Francisco: Jossey-Bass.

Aguirre, A., Jr. (2004). *Diversity versus affirmative action: A critical race theory story.* Paper presented at the national symposium on multicontextuality, unity, and diversity in a pluralistic society at the University of New Mexico. September, Albuquerque, NM.

Aguirre, A., Jr. (2005). The personal narrative as academic storytelling: A Chicano's search for presence and voice in academe. *International Journal of Qualitative Studies in Education, 18,* 147–163.

Aguirre, A., Jr. (forthcoming). Diversity, social capital, and leadership practices: Building inclusive learning organizations. *International Journal of Management and Decision Making.*

Aguirre, A., Jr., and Martinez, R. (2002). Leadership practices and diversity in higher education: Transitional and transformational frameworks. *Journal of Leadership Studies, 8,* 53–62.

Aguirre, A., Jr., and Martinez, R. (2003a). The diversity rationale in higher education: An overview of the contemporary legal context. *Social Justice, 30,* 138–152.

Aguirre, A., Jr., and Martinez, R. (2003b). *The organizational response to diversity: Leading for diversity versus diversifying leadership.* Paper presented at the 8th Annual Conference of the People of Color in Predominantly White Institutions at the University of Nebraska. November, Lincoln, Nebraska.

Alderfer, C. (1985). Taking ourselves seriously as researchers. In D. Berg and K. Smith (Eds.), *Exploring clinical matters for social research* (pp. 35–70). Beverly Hills, CA: Sage.

Alderfer, C., and Thomas, D. (1988). The significance of race and ethnicity for understanding organizational behavior. *International Review of Industrial and Organizational Psychology, 1,* 1–41.

Alire, C. (2001). Diversity and leadership: The color of leadership. *Journal of Library Administration, 32,* 95–109.

Allison, M. (1999). Organizational barriers to diversity in the workplace. *Journal of Leisure Research, 31,* 78–101.

Amaral, A., and Magalhã, A. (2003). The triple crisis of the university and its reinvention. *Higher Education Policy, 16,* 253–293.

American Association of University Women. (2005). *The (un)changing face of the Ivy League.* Washington, DC: American Association of University Women.

Andrews, H., and Cavan, J. (2002). Community services impact college leadership, diversity, and student services. *Community College Journal, 72,* 29–32.

Arenson, K. (2005, March 1). Little advance is seen at Ivies in the hiring of women and minorities. *New York Times,* p. A13.

Argyris, C., and Schön, D. (1978). *Organizational learning: A theory of action perspective.* Reading, MA: Addison-Wesley.

Argyris, C., and Schön, D. (1996). *Organizational learning II.* Reading, MA: Addison-Wesley.

Armour, S. (2003, July 21). Debate revived on workplace diversity. *USA Today,* p. A1.

Arocena, R., and Sutz, J. (2005). Latin American universities: From an original revolution to an uncertain transition. *Higher Education, 50,* 573–592.

Arthur, J., and Shapiro, A. (Eds.). (1995). *Campus wars: Multiculturalism and the politics of difference.* Boulder, CO: Westview Press.

Association of American Colleges and Universities. (n.d.). *Reasons for hope: Promising practices from the campus diversity initiative.* Washington, DC: Association of American Colleges and Universities.

Astin, A., and Astin, H. (2000). *Leadership reconsidered: Engaging higher education in social change.* Battle Creek, MI: Kellogg Foundation.

Avolio, B. J., Waldman, D. A., and Yammarino, F. J. (1991). Leading in the 1990s: The four I's of transformational leadership. *Journal of European Industrial Training, 15,* 9–16.

Ayers, D. (2005). Organizational climate in its semiotic aspect: A postmodern community college undergoes renewal. *Community College Review, 33,* 1–21.

Baker, O. (1996). The managing diversity movement: Origins, status, and challenges. In B. Bowser and R. Hunt (Eds.), *Impacts of racism on white Americans* (2nd ed.) (pp. 139–156). Thousand Oaks, CA: Sage.

Baldridge, J. V., Curtis, D. V., Ecker, G., and Riley, G. L. (1977). Diversity in higher education: Professional autonomy. *Journal of Higher Education, 48,* 367–388.

Banks, J. (1995). Multicultural education and curriculum transformation. *Journal of Negro Education, 64,* 390–490.

Bass, B. (1985). *Leadership and performance beyond expectations.* New York: Free Press.

Bass, B. (1999). Two decades of research and development in transformational leadership. *European Journal of Work and Organizational Psychology, 8,* 9–33.

Battin, P. (1997). Diversity and leadership: Mentoring builds leaders of the future. *Cause/Effect, 20,* 15–17.

Beane, J. (1998). Reclaiming a democratic purpose for education. *Educational Leadership, 56,* 8–11.

Beck, C. (1993). Postmodernism, pedagogy, and philosophy of education. *Philosophy of Education, 27,* 1–13.

Behar-Horenstein, L., and Amatea, E. (1996). Changing worlds, changing paradigms: Redesigning administrative practice for more turbulent times. *Educational Horizons, 75,* 27–35.

Benjamin, M. (1996). *Cultural diversity, educational equity and the transformation of higher education: Group profiles as a guide to policy and programming.* Westport, CT: Praeger.

Bensimon, E. (1989a). A feminist reinterpretation of presidents' definitions of leadership. *Peabody Journal of Education, 66,* 143–156.

Bensimon, E. (1989b). The meaning of "good presidential leadership": A frame analysis. *Review of Higher Education, 12,* 107–123.

Bensimon, E. (1995). Total quality management in the academy: A rebellious reading. *Harvard Educational Review, 65,* 593–701.

Bensimon, E. M., Neumann, A., and Birnbaum, R. (1989). *Making sense of administrative leadership: The "L" word in higher education.* ASHE-ERIC Higher Education Report, No. 1. Washington, DC: School of Education and Human Development, The George Washington University.

Bergquist, W. (1993). *The post-modern organization: Mastering the art of irreversible change.* San Francisco: Jossey-Bass.

Bergquist, W. (1998). The postmodern challenge: Changing our community colleges. *New Directions for Community Colleges, 102,* 87–99.

Bernard, E. (2005). Teaching the N-word. *American Scholar, 74,* 46–59.

Berry, M. (1996). Vindicating Martin Luther King, Jr.: The road to a color-blind society. *Journal of Negro History, 81,* 137–144.

Bess, J., and Goldman, P. (2001). Leadership ambiguity in universities and K–12 schools and the limits of contemporary leadership theory. *Leadership Quarterly, 12,* 419–450.

Birnbaum, R. (1983). *Maintaining diversity in higher education.* San Francisco: Jossey-Bass.

Birnbaum, R. (1988). Consistency and diversity in the goals of campus leaders. *Review of Higher Education, 12,* 17–30.

Birnbaum, R. (2000a). The life cycle of academic management fads. *Journal of Higher Education, 71,* 1–16.

Birnbaum, R. (2000b). *Management fads in higher education.* San Francisco: Jossey-Bass.

Blau, P. (1973). *The organization of academic work.* New York: Wiley.

Blauner, R. (1972). *Racial oppression in America.* New York: Harper & Row.

Bloland, H. (1995). Postmodernism and higher education. *Journal of Higher Education, 66,* 521–559.

Bloom, A. (1987). *The closing of the American mind.* New York: Simon & Schuster.

Bollag, B. (2005, July 29). Classroom drama. *Chronicle of Higher Education,* pp. A12–A14.

Bond, M., and Pyle, J. (1998). Diversity dilemmas at work. *Journal of Management Inquiry, 7,* 252–270.

Bonilla-Silva, E. (2003a). "New racism," color-blind racism, and the future of whiteness in America. In A. Doane and E. Bonilla-Silva (Eds.), *White out: The continuing significance of racism* (pp. 271–284). New York: Routledge.

Bonilla-Silva, E. (2003b). *Racism without racists: Color-blind racism and the persistence of racial inequality in the United States.* Lanham, MD: Rowman & Littlefield.

Bonilla-Silva, E., Lewis, A., and Embrick, D. (2004). "I did not get that job because of a black man . . .": The story lines and testimonies of color-blind racism. *Sociological Forum, 19,* 555–581.

Borkowski, F. (1988). The university president's role in establishing an institutional climate to encourage minority participation in higher education. *Peabody Journal of Education, 66,* 32–45.

Bowen, W., Bok, D., and Burkhart, G. (1999, January/February). A report card on diversity: Lessons for business from higher education. *Harvard Business Review,* 139–149.

Bower, B. (2002). Campus life for faculty of color: Still strangers after all these years? *New Directions for Community Colleges, 118,* 79–87.

Brandt, R. (1994). On educating for diversity: A conversation with James A. Banks. *Educational Leadership, 51,* 28–31.

Bray, N. J. (2003). *Differences among faculty members' perceptions of norms for academic deans.* Paper presented at the 28th Annual Conference of the Association for the Study of Higher Education, November, Portland, OR.

Brayboy, B.M.J. (2003). The implementation of diversity in predominantly white colleges and universities. *Journal of Black Studies, 34,* 72–86.

Bridges, B., Holmes, M., Morelon, C., and Williams, J. (2004). *African American and Hispanic student engagement at minority serving and predominantly white institutions.* Paper presented at the annual meeting of the Association for the Study of Higher Education, November, Kansas City, MO.

Bringle, R., and Hatcher, J. (1996). Implementing service learning in higher education. *Journal of Higher Education, 67,* 221–239.

Brown, C. (1998). Campus diversity: Presidents as leaders. *College Student Affairs Journal, 18,* 84–93.

Brown, L. (2004). Diversity: The challenge for higher education. *Race, Ethnicity and Education, 7,* 21–34.

Brown, M., and others. (2003). *Whitewashing race: The myth of a color-blind society.* Berkeley: University of California Press.

Bunzel, J. (2001). The diversity dialogues in higher education. *Fordham Urban Law Review, 29,* 489–512.

Burns, J. (1978). *Leadership.* New York: Harper & Row.

Burt, R. (1992). *Structural holes: The social structure of competition.* Cambridge, MA: Harvard University Press.

Burt, R. (2000). The network structure of social capital. In R. Sutton and B. Staw (Eds.), *Research in organizational behavior* (pp. 345–423). Greenwich, CT: JAI Press.

Butler, J., and Walter, J. (Eds.). (1991). *Transforming the curriculum: Ethnic studies and women's studies.* Albany: SUNY Press.

Byrkjeflot, H., and Fligstein, N. (1996). The logic of employment systems. In J. Baron, D. Grusk, and D. Treiman (Eds.), *Social differentiation and social inequity* (pp. 11–37). Boulder, CO: Westview Press.

Calderon, H., and Saldivar, J. (Eds.). (1991). *Criticism in the borderlands: Studies in Chicano literature, culture, and ideology.* Durham, NC: Duke University Press.

Carchidi, D., and Peterson, M. (2000). Emerging organizational structures. *Planning for Higher Education, 28,* 1–15.

Castenell, L., and Tarule, J. (Eds.). (1997). *The minority voice in educational reform: An analysis by minority and women college of education deans.* Greenwich, CT: Ablex.

Center on Diversity and Community. (2002, January). University of Oregon Campus climate on diversity: Executive summary of survey results. Eugene, OR: University of Oregon Center on Diversity and Community.

Chaffee, E., and Tierney, W. (1988). *Collegiate culture and leadership strategies.* Washington, DC: American Council on Education.

Chahin, J. (1993). *Leadership, diversity and the campus community.* Paper presented at the national conference of the American Association for Higher Education, March, Washington, DC.

Chalmers, V. (1987). White out: Multicultural performances in a progressive school. In M. Fine, L. Weiss, L. Powell, and L. Wong (Eds.), *Off-white readings on race, power, and society* (pp. 66–76). New York: Routledge.

Chan, S., and Wang, L. (1991). Racism and the model minority: Asian-Americans in higher education. In P. Altbach and K. Lomotey (Eds.), *The racial crisis in American higher education* (pp. 43–67). Albany: SUNY Press.

Chang, M. (2002). Preservation or transformation: Where's the real educational discourse on diversity? *Review of Higher Education, 25,* 125–140.

Chang, M. (2005). Reconsidering the diversity rationale. *Liberal Education, 91,* 6–13.

Chang, M., Witt, D., Jones, J., and Hakuta, K. (2003). *Compelling interest: Examining the evidence on racial dynamics in colleges and universities.* Palo Alto, CA: Stanford University.

Chen, C., and Vilsor, E. (1996). New directions for research and practice in diversity leadership. *Leadership Quarterly, 7,* 285–302.

Chesler, M., Lewis, A., and Crowfoot, J. (2005). *Challenging racism in higher education: Promoting justice.* New York: Rowman & Littlefield.

Clark, B. (1972). The organizational saga in higher education. *Administrative Science Quarterly, 17,* 178–184.

Clark, C. (2002). Effective multicultural curriculum transformation across disciplines. *Multicultural Perspectives, 4,* 37–46.

Cohen, M., and March, J. (1986). *Leadership in an organized anarchy.* Cambridge, MA: Harvard Business School.

Collins, R., and Johnson, J. (1988). One institution's success in increasing the number of minority faculty. *Peabody Journal of Education, 66,* 71–76.

Colon, A. (1991). Race relations on campus: An administrative perspective. In P. Altbach and K. Lomotey (Eds.), *The racial crisis in American higher education* (pp. 69–88). Albany: SUNY Press.

Colon, A. (2003). Black studies: Historical background, modern origins, and development priorities for the early twenty first century. *Western Journal of Black Studies, 27,* 145–156.

Colvin, G. (1999, July 19). The 50 best companies for Asians, blacks, and Hispanics: Companies that pursue diversity outperform the S&P 500. Coincidence? *Fortune,* pp. 53–54.

Conger, J. (1999). Charismatic and transformational leadership in organizations: An insider's perspective on those developing streams of research. *Leadership Quarterly, 10,* 145–180.

Conrad, C. (1978). A grounded theory of academic change. *Sociology of Education, 51,* 101–112.

Contreras, A. R. (1998). Leading from the margins in the ivory tower. In L. Valverde and L. Castenell (Eds.), *The multicultural campus: Strategies for transforming higher education* (pp. 137–166). Walnut Creek, CA: AltaMira Press.

Coopey, J. (1995). The learning organization, power, politics and ideology. *Management Learning, 26,* 193–213.

Coppieters, P. (2005). Turning schools into learning organizations. *European Journal of Teacher Education, 28,* 129–139.

Corrigan, R. (1995). Diversity, public perception and institutional voice. *Liberal Education, 8,* 20–31.

Cullen, J. (1999). Socially constructed learning: A commentary on the concept of the learning organization. *Learning Organization, 6,* 45–52.

Davidson, M. (1999). The value of being included: An examination of diversity change initiatives in organizations. *Performance Improvement Quarterly, 12,* 164–180.

Davis, E., and Davis, D. (1999). The university presidency: Do evaluations make a difference? *Journal of Personnel Evaluation in Education, 13,* 119–140.

Denton, K. (1997). Down with diversity (at least some of it): A case for cultural identity. *Empowerment in Organizations, 5,* 170–175.

Diamond, R. (Ed.). (2002). *Field guide to academic leadership: A publication of the National Academy for Academic Leadership.* San Francisco: Jossey-Bass.

Dillard, A. (2004). How the new black elite peddles conservatism. *New Labor Forum, 13,* 31–38.

DiTomaso, N., and Hooijberg, R. (1996). Diversity and the demands of leadership. *Leadership Quarterly, 7,* 163–187.

Dooris, M., Kelley, J., and Trainer, J. (2004). Strategic planning in higher education. *New Directions for Institutional Research, 123,* 5–11.

Dowdy, K. (1998). *Noises in the attic: The legacy of expectations in the academy.* Paper presented at an annual meeting of the American Educational Research Association, April, San Diego, CA.

Dunham, K. (2002, January 29). Isolation at top hurts minorities when layoffs hit. *Wall Street Journal,* p. B1.

Durhams, S. (2000, September 20). UW–Madison doctors photo to stress diversity: Picture of minority student digitally inserted into shot on application bulletin. *Milwaukee Journal Sentinel,* p. B1.

Duryea, E. (2000). Evolution of university organization. In M. C. Brown II (Ed.), *Organization and governance in higher education* (5th ed.) (pp. 3–15). Boston: Pearson Custom Publishing.

Easterby-Smith, M., Araujo, L., and Burgoyne, J. (Eds.). (1999). *Organizational learning and the learning organization: Developments in theory and practice.* Thousand Oaks, CA: Sage.

Eckstein, S. (1976). The irony of organization: Resource and regulatory. *British Journal of Sociology, 27,* 150–164.

English, F. (1997). The cupboard is bare: The postmodern critique of educational administration. *Journal of School Leadership, 7,* 4–26.

English, F. (1998). The postmodern turn in educational administration: Apostrophic or catastrophic development? *Journal of School Leadership, 8,* 426–447.

Essed, P. (2004). Cloning amongst professors: Normativities and imagined homogeneities. *NORA: Nordic Journal of Women's Studies, 12,* 113–122.

Etzioni, A. (1965). Dual leadership in complex organizations. *American Sociological Review, 30,* 688–698.

Ewell, P. (1985). *Transformation leadership for improving student outcomes.* NCHEMS Monograph 6. Boulder, CO: National Center for Higher Education Management Systems.

Farmer, E. (1997). The need for more culturally diverse leaders in postsecondary technical education: A challenge for community colleges. *Journal of Industrial Teacher Education, 35,* 109–112.

Fenelon, J. (2003). Race, research, and tenure. *Journal of Black Studies, 34,* 87–100.

Fisher, A. (2004, November 15). How you can do better on diversity. *Fortune,* p. 60.

Fletcher, M. (2002, May 15). Use of race in law school entry upheld. *Washington Post,* p. A1.

Foldy, E. (2004). Learning from diversity: A theoretical explanation. *Public Administration Review, 64,* 529–538.

Ford, J., and Harding, N. (2004). We went looking for an organization but could find only the metaphysics of its presence. *Sociology, 38,* 815-830.

Freed, J., and Klugman, M. (1996, June). *Higher education institutions as learning organizations: The quality principles and practices in higher education.* Paper presented at the annual meeting of the Association for the Study of Higher Education, Richmond, VA.

Fujita, E. (1994). A good college president: The constituent view. *Journal of Personnel Evaluation in Education, 8,* 75–91.

Fuller, B. (1976). A framework for academic planning. *Journal of Higher Education, 47,* 65–77.

Fullinwider, R. (1997). Diversity and affirmative action. *Report from the Institute for Philosophy and Public Policy, 17,* 1–8.

Gabor, A. (2000). *The capitalist philosophers: The geniuses of modern business: Their lives, times, and ideas.* New York: Times Books.

Galis, L. (1993). Merely academic diversity. *Journal of Higher Education, 64,* 93–101.

Gallos, J. (2002). The dean's squeeze: The myths and realities of academic leadership in the middle. *Academy of Management Learning and Education, 1,* 174–184.

Garcia, M. (Ed.). (2000). *Succeeding in an academic career: A guide for faculty of color.* Westport, CT: Greenwood Press.

Gephart, R. (1996). Postmodernism and the future history of management. *Journal of Management History, 2,* 90–96.

Giles, C., and Hargreaves, A. (2006). The sustainability of innovative schools as learning organizations and professional learning communities during standardized reform. *Educational Administration Quarterly, 42,* 124–156.

Golembiewski, R., and Kuhnert, K. (1994). Management 2000: Looking forward to enhance tomorrow's practice. *International Journal of Public Administration, 17,* 459–464.

Graduate Employees and Student Organizations. (2005, February). *The (un)changing face of the Ivy League.* New Haven, CT: Yale University.

Green, D. (2004). Fighting the battle for racial diversity: A case study of Michigan's institutional responses to *Gratz* and *Grutter. Educational Policy, 18,* 733–751.

Green, M. (Ed.). (1988). *Leaders for a new era: Strategies for higher education.* New York: Macmillan.

Gregory, M. (1996). Developing effective college leadership for the management of educational change. *Leadership and Organizational Development Journal, 17,* 46–52.

Gurin, P., Lehman, J., and Lewis, E. (2004). *Defending diversity: Affirmative action at the University of Michigan.* Ann Arbor: University of Michigan.

Gutierrez, M., Castaneda, C., and Katsinas, S. (2002). Latino leadership in community colleges: Issues and challenges. *Community College Journal of Research and Practice, 26,* 297–314.

Hale, F. (Ed.). (2004). *What makes racial diversity work in higher education: Academic leaders present successful policies and strategies.* Herndon, VA: Stylus.

Hall, R. (1996). *Organizations: Structures, processes, and outcomes* (6th ed.). Englewood Cliffs, NJ: Prentice Hall.

Haro, R. (1992). Lessons from practice. *Change, 24,* 54–58.

Hartley, D. (2004). Management, leadership, and the emotional order of the school. *Journal of Education Policy, 19,* 583–594.

Hays, C. (2000, January 4). Mindful of its public image, Coke strives to retain black executive. *New York Times,* p. C1.

Heller, S. (1989, November 8). Press for campus diversity leading to more closed minds, say critics. *Chronicle of Higher Education,* pp. A13, A22.

Herbert, A. (1974). The minority administrator: Problems, prospects, and challenges. *Public Administration Review, 34,* 556–563.

Higgs, M. (1996). Overcoming the problems of cultural differences to establish success for international management teams. *Team Performance Management: An International Journal, 2,* 36–43.

Hill, B., Green, M., and Eckel, P. (2001). *What governing boards need to know and do about institutional change.* Washington, DC: American Council on Education.

Hooijberg, R., and DiTomaso, N. (1996). Leadership in and of demographically diverse organizations. *Leadership Quarterly, 7,* 1–19.

Hoover, J. (2002). Making ourselves useful: Crossing academic and social boundaries. *American Behavioral Scientist, 45,* 1135–1144.

Hrabowski, F. (2004). Leadership for a new age: Higher education's role in producing minority leaders. *Liberal Education, 90,* 26–33.

Hubbard, E. (Ed.). (1998). *Best practices in institutional planning for diversity.* Boulder, CO: Western Interstate Commission for Higher Education.

Hu-Dehart, E. (2000). The diversity project: Institutionalizing multiculturalism or managing differences? *Academe, 86,* 38–42.

Hudson, J. (1995). Simple justice: Affirmative action and American racism in historical perspective. *Black Scholar, 25,* 16–23.

Humphreys, D. (2000). Diversity plan trends aim to meet 21st century challenges. *Black Issues in Higher Education, 16,* 34–36.

Hurtado, S., Milem, J., Clayton-Pederson, A., and Allen, W. (1999). *Enacting diverse learning environments: Improving the climate for racial/ethnic diversity in higher education.* ASHE-ERIC Higher Education Report, Vol. 26, No. 8. Washington, DC: Graduate School of Education and Human Development, The George Washington University.

Hyter, M. (2004). Diversity programs to grow. *Journal for Quality and Participation, 27,* 52.

Ibarra, R. (2001). *Beyond affirmative action: Reframing the context of higher education.* Madison: University of Wisconsin Press.

Ingle, G. (2005). Will your campus diversity initiative work? *Academe, 91,* 13–16.

Institute for Higher Education Policy. (2004). *Leading the way to America's future: A monograph about the launch and implementation of the Kellogg MSI leadership fellows program, 2002–2004.* Washington, DC: Institute for Higher Education Policy.

Jackson, J. (2006). Hiring practices of African American males in academic leadership positions at American colleges and universities: An employment trends and disparate impact analysis. *Teachers College Record, 108,* 316–338.

Jacobs, K. (2002, February 10). More companies seek diversity as internal bias suits increase. *Houston Chronicle,* p. D2.

Jacobs, L., Cintron, J., and Canton, C. (Eds.). (2002). *The politics of survival in academia: Narratives of inequality, resilience, and success.* Boulder, CO: Rowman & Littlefield.

Jaffee, D. (2001). *Organization theory: Tension and change.* New York: McGraw-Hill.

Johnsrud, L., and Sadao, K. (1998). The common experience of "otherness": Ethnic and racial minority faculty. *Review of Higher Education, 21,* 315–342.

Johnston, B. (1996). Types of educational leadership in a postindustrial society. *Urban Review, 28,* 213–232.

Judkins, B., and LaHurd, R. (1999). Building community from diversity: Addressing the changing demographics of academia and society. *American Behavioral Scientist, 42,* 786–799.

Julius, D., Baldridge, J., and Pfeffer, J. (1999). A memo from Machiavelli. *Journal of Higher Education, 70,* 113–133.

Jurik, N., Blumenthal, J., Smith, B., and Portillos, E. (2000). Organizational cooptation or social change? A critical perspective on community criminal justice partnerships. *Journal of Contemporary Criminal Justice, 16,* 293–320.

Justiz, M., Wilson, R., and Bjork, L. (Eds.). (1994). *Minorities in higher education.* Phoenix, AZ: Oryx Press.

Karen, D. (1991). The politics of class, race, and gender: Access to higher education in the United States, 1960–1986. *American Journal of Education, 99,* 208–237.

Keller, G. (1983). *Academic strategy.* Baltimore: Johns Hopkins University Press.

Keough, T., and Tobin, B. (2001). *Postmodern leadership and the policy lexicon: From theory, proxy to practice.* Paper presented at the Pan-Canadian Education Research Agenda Symposium, May, Quebec City, QC.

Kerr, C., and Gade, M. (1986). *The many lives of academic presidents: Time, place and character.* Washington, DC: Association of Governing Boards of Colleges and Universities.

Ketchen, D., and others. (1997). Organizational configurations and performance: A meta-analysis. *Academy of Management Journal, 40,* 223–240.

Keup, J., Walker, A., Astin, H., and Lindholm, J. (2001). *Organizational culture and transformational change.* Washington, DC: School of Education and Human Development, The George Washington University.

Kezar, A. (2000). Pluralistic leadership: Incorporating diverse voices. *Journal of Higher Education, 71,* 722–743.

Kezar, A. (2001). *Understanding and facilitating organizational change in the 21st century: Recent research and conceptualizations.* ASHE-ERIC Higher Education Report, Vol. 28, No. 4. San Francisco: Jossey-Bass.

Kezar, A. (2002). Expanding notions of leadership to capture pluralistic voices: Positionality theory in practice. *Journal of College Student Development, 43,* 558–578.

Kezar, A. (2005). What campuses need to know about organizational learning and the learning organization. *New Directions for Higher Education, 131,* 7–22.

Killian, L. (1990). Race relations and the nineties: Where are the dreams of the sixties? *Social Forces, 69,* 1–13.

Kohn, M. (2005). Frederick Douglass' master-slave dialectic. *Journal of Politics, 67,* 497–514.

Kotler, P., and Murphy, P. (1981). Strategic planning for higher education. *Journal of Higher Education, 52,* 470–489.

Kouzes, J., and Posner, B. (1989). *The leadership challenge: How to get extraordinary things done in organizations.* San Francisco: Jossey-Bass.

Kozlowski, S., and Doherty, M. (1989). Integration of climate and leadership. *Journal of Applied Psychology, 74,* 546–553.

Kramer, M., and Weiner, S. (1994). *Dialogues for diversity: Community and ethnicity on campus.* Phoenix, AZ: Oryx Press.

LaBelle, T., and Ward, C. (1996). *Ethnic studies and multiculturalism.* Albany: SUNY Press.

Lamb, S. (1999). The Holmes scholars network: A networking mentoring program of the Holmes partnership. *Peabody Journal of Education, 74,* 150–162.

Law, I., Phillips, D., and Turney, L. (Eds.). (2004). *Institutional racism in higher education.* Sterling, VA: Trentham Books Limited.

Leatherman, C. (1993, December 1). Professors protest changes at James Madison U. *Chronicle of Higher Education,* p. A20.

Leon, D. (Ed.). (2005). Lessons in leadership: Executive leadership programs for advancing diversity in higher education. New York: Elsevier.

Levin, J. (1998). Presidential influence, leadership succession, and multiple interpretations of organizational change. *Review of Higher Education, 21,* 405–425.

Lewis, A., Chesler, M., and Forman, T. (2000). The impact of color-blind ideologies on students of color: Intergroup relations at a predominantly white university. *Journal of Negro Education, 69,* 74–91.

Lewis, J. (2002, March 28). Diversity objectives should be linked to company's overall business strategy. *The Birmingham Times,* p. A2.

Lindsey, R., Robins, K., and Terrell, R. (1999). *Cultural proficiency: A manual for school leaders.* Thousand Oaks, CA: Corwin Press.

Lopez-Mulnix, E., and Mulnix, M. (2006). Models of excellence in multicultural colleges and universities. *Journal of Hispanic Higher Education, 5,* 4–21.

Losco, J., and Fife, B. (Eds.). (2000). *Higher education in transition: The challenges of a new millennium.* Westport, CT: Bergin & Garvey.

Lowe, E. (1999). Promise and dilemma: Perspectives on racial diversity and higher education. In E. Lowe (Ed.), *Promise and dilemma* (pp. 3–43). Princeton, NJ: Princeton University Press.

Lurie, T. (1998, Winter). Campus diversity gets high marks in poll. *Ford Foundation Reports.* New York: Ford Foundation.

Mabokela, R., and Madsen, J. (2003). "Color-blind" leadership and intergroup conflict. *Journal of School Leadership, 13,* 130–158.

Martin, J. (2003). Multiple intelligences and business diversity. *Journal of Career Assessment, 11,* 187–204.

Martin, W. (1982). *A college of character: Renewing the purpose and content of college education.* San Francisco: Jossey-Bass.

Martinez, R. (2005). Latino demographic and institutional issues in higher education: Implications for leadership development. In D. Leon (Ed.), *Lessons in leadership: Executive leadership programs for advancing diversity in higher education* (pp. 17–55). New York: Elsevier.

Masland, A. (2000). Organizational culture in the study of higher education. In M. C. Brown II (Ed.), *Organization and governance in higher education* (5th ed.) (pp. 145–152). Boston: Pearson Custom Publishing.

Matczynski, T., Lasley, T. J., and Haberman, M. (1989). The deanship: How faculty evaluate performance. *Journal of Teacher Education, 40,* 10–14.

McMillen, L. (1990, September 19). Ford fund gives $1.6 million to 19 colleges to keep up with demographic changes. *Chronicle of Higher Education,* p. A37.

McNulty, M. (1995). Campus leadership and American pluralism. *Liberal Education, 81,* 44–47.

Merritt, J. (2002, March 11). Wanted: A campus that looks like America. *Business Week,* pp. 56–58.

Minor, J., and Tierney, W. (2005). The danger of deference: A case of polite governance. *Teachers College Record, 107,* 137–156.

Mirchandani, R. (2005). Postmodernism and sociology: From the epistemological to the empirical. *Sociological Theory, 23,* 86–115.

Mitchell, C., and Kumar, R. (2001). The development of administrative discourse in a pluralistic society. *Journal of Educational Administration and Foundations, 15,* 47–67.

Morrill, R. (2000). The use of indicators in the strategic management of universities. *Higher Education Management, 12,* 105–114.

Morris, L. (2005). Dramatic changes in faculty demographics. *Innovative Higher Education, 30,* 85–87.

Morris, V. C. (1981). *Deaning: Middle management in academe.* Urbana, IL: University of Illinois Press.

Morrow, G., Burris-Kitchen, D., and Der-Karabetian, A. (2000). Assessing campus climate of cultural diversity: A focus on focus groups. *College Student Journal, 34,* 589–602.

Moss, W. (2004). *Creative conflict in African American thought: Frederick Douglass, Alexander Crummell, Booker T. Washington, W.E.B. DuBois, and Marcus Garvey.* New York: Cambridge University Press.

Munoz, J., Jasis, R., Young, P., and McLaren, P. (2004). The hidden curriculum of domestication. *Urban Review, 36,* 169–187.

Murrell, A., Crosby, F., and Ely, R. (Eds.). (1999). *Mentoring dilemmas: Developmental relationships within multicultural organizations.* Mahwah, NJ: Erlbaum.

Nelsen, A. (1994). *Crucial practices for diversity: A project report.* University Park, PA: Alliance for Undergraduate Education.

Neumann, A. (1988). The meaning of good faculty leadership. *Leadership Abstracts (Worldwide Web Edition), 5.* Retrieved from http://www.league.org/publication/abstracts/leadership/labs0388.html.

Niemann, Y., and Dovidio, J. (1998). Tenure, race/ethnicity and attitudes toward affirmative action: A matter of self-interest? *Sociological Perspectives, 41,* 783–796.

Niemann, Y., and Dovidio, J. (2005). Affirmative action and job satisfaction: Understanding underlying processes. *Journal of Social Issues, 61,* 507–523.

Niemann, Y., and Maruyama, G. (2005). Inequities in higher education: Issues and promising practices in a world ambivalent about affirmative action. *Journal of Social Issues, 61,* 407–426.

Nkomo, S. (1992). The emperor has no clothes: Revisiting "race in organizations." *Academy of Management Review, 17,* 487–513.

O'Donnell, L., and Green-Merritt, E. (1997). Empowering minorities to impact the established culture in Eurocentric institutions of higher learning. *ERIC Clearinghouse Document* (ED 412 823).

Ogilvy, J. (1963, Summer). The problems of a president. *Colorado Quarterly,* pp. 55–63.

O'Toole, L., Jr., and Meier, K. (2003). *Desperately seeking Selznick: Cooptation and the dark side of public management in networks*. Paper presented at the National Public Management Research Association Conference, October, Washington, DC.

Padeken, M., and Stein, W. (Eds.). (2003). *The renaissance of American Indian higher education: Capturing the dream*. Mahwah, NJ: Erlbaum.

Padilla, R., and Martinez, R. (2005). Personal stories, voice and presence in academe: A dialogical response to Aguirre. *International Journal of Qualitative Studies in Education, 18*, 199–220.

Padilla, R., and Montiel, M. (1998). *Debatable diversity: Critical dialogues on change in American universities*. New York: Rowman & Littlefield.

Parloff, R. (2002, February 8). *Bakke* is as good a fudge as any in achieving racial diversity in colleges. *Fulton County Daily Report*, p. 1.

Pavel, M. (2003). Double-loop diversity: Applying adult learning theory to the cultivation of diverse educational climates in higher education. *Innovative Higher Education, 28*, 35–47.

Perea, J., Delgado, R., Harris, A., and Wildman, S. (2000). *Race and races: Cases and resources for a diverse America*. St. Paul: West Group.

Peterson, M. (1985). Emerging developments in postsecondary organization theory and research: Fragmentation or integration? *Educational Researcher, 14*, 5–12.

Peterson, M., Dill, D., and Mets, L. (1997). *Planning and management for a changing environment: A handbook on redesigning postsecondary institutions*. San Francisco: Jossey-Bass.

Peterson, M., and Spencer, M. (1990). Understanding academic culture and climate. *New Directions for Institutional Research, 68*, 3–18.

Pettigrew, A. (1979). On studying organizational cultures. *Administrative Science Quarterly, 24*, 570–581.

Phillips, W., and Blumberg, R. (1982). Tokenism and organizational change: Theoretical examination of an aspect of race relations in educational context. *ERIC Clearinghouse Document* (ED 213 815).

Platt, M. (1993). Beyond the canon, with great difficulties. *Social Justice, 20*, 72–81.

Pope, M. (2002). Community college mentoring: Minority student perceptions. *Community College Review, 30*, 31–45.

Pounder, J. (2001). "New leadership" and university organizational effectiveness: Exploring the relationship. *Leadership and Organizational Development Journal, 22*, 281–290.

Ramirez, S. (2000). The new cultural diversity and title VII. *Michigan Journal of Race and Law, 6*, 127–179.

Rendon, L., and Hope, R. (Eds.). (1996). *Educating a new majority: Transforming America's educational system for diversity*. San Francisco: Jossey-Bass.

Richardson, R. C., and Skinner, E. F. (1991). *Achieving quality and diversity*. Washington, DC: American Council on Education/Macmillan Publishing Company.

Roach, R. (1999). Blacks in crimson. *Black Issues In Higher Education, 15*, 32–33.

Rogers, J. (1992, Summer). Leadership development for the 90s: Incorporating emergent paradigm perspectives. *NASPA Journal*, pp. 243–251.

Rosser, V. J. (2003). Using multilevel SEM to study leadership effectiveness in higher education. In J. Smart (ed.), *Higher education: Handbook of theory and research* (Vol. 18) (pp. 389–420). London, UK: Kluwer Academic Publishers.

Rosser, V., Johnsrud, L., and Heck, R. (2003). Academic deans and directors: Assessing their effectiveness from individual and institutional perspectives. *Journal of Higher Education, 74,* 1–25.

Rost, J. (1991). *Leadership in the 21st century.* New York: Praeger.

Rost, J. (1993, November). Leadership development in the new millennium. *Journal of Leadership Studies,* pp. 91–110.

Rothman, S., Lipset, S., and Nevitte, N. (2002). Diversity and affirmative action: The state of campus opinion. *Academic Questions, 15,* 52–66.

Sacks, D., and Thiel, P. (1995). Multiculturalism and the decline of Stanford. *Academic Questions, 8,* 58–67.

Sandham, J. (1997). Affirmative action is key to diversity, admissions officers say. *Education Week, 17,* 12.

Santiago, I. (1996). Increasing the Latino leadership pipeline: Institutional and organizational strategies. *New Directions for Community Colleges, 94,* 25–38.

Sappal, P. (2003, October 28). Schools get creative to hike minority MBA enrollment. *Wall Street Journal On-Line.* Retrieved October 28, 2005, from www.wsj.com.

Sawires, J., and Peacock, M. (2000). Symbolic racism and voting behavior on proposition 209. *Journal of Applied Social Psychology, 30,* 2092–2099.

Selznick, P. (1948). Foundations of the theory of organization. *American Sociological Review, 13,* 25–35.

Selznick, P. (1949). *TVA and the grassroots.* Berkeley: University of California Press.

Selznick, P. (1957). *Leadership in administration.* New York: Harper & Row.

Senge, P. (1990). *The fifth discipline: The art and practice of the learning organization.* New York: Doubleday.

Shapiro, L., and Nunez, W. (2000). Strategy planning synergy. *Planning for Higher Education, 30,* 27–34.

Sinclair, A. (2002). *Doing leadership differently.* Paper presented at the annual meeting of the Australian Association of Alumni and Development Professionals in Education, September, Melbourne, Australia.

Sinclair, A. (2004). Journey around leadership. *Discourse: Studies in the cultural politics of education, 25,* 7–19.

Smith, D. (2000). Organizing for diversity: Fundamental issues. In C. Turner, M. Garcia, A. Nora, and L. Rendon (Eds.), *Racial and ethnic diversity in higher education* (pp. 532–541). Needham Heights, MA: Simon & Schuster Custom Publishing.

Smith, D., Turner, C., Osei-Kofi, N., and Richards, S. (2004). Interrupting the usual: Successful strategies for hiring diverse faculty. *Journal of Higher Education, 75,* 133–160.

Smith, J., Smith, W., and Markham, S. (2000). Diversity issues in mentoring academic faculty. *Journal of Career Development, 26,* 251–262.

Smith, W., Altbach, P., and Lomotey, K. (Eds.). (2002). *The racial crisis in American higher education: Continuing challenges for the twenty-first century.* Albany: SUNY Press.

Solorzano, D., Ceja, M., and Yosso, T. (2000). Critical race theory, racial microaggressions, and campus racial climate: The experiences of African American college students. *Journal of Negro Education, 69,* 60–73.

Springer, L. (1996). Attitudes toward campus diversity: Participation in a racial or cultural awareness workshop. *Review of Higher Education, 20,* 53–68.

Stadtman, V. (1980). *Academic adaptations.* San Francisco: Jossey-Bass.

Steers, R., and Black, J. (1994). *Organizational behavior* (5th ed.). New York: HarperCollins College Publishers.

Steinberg, J. (2002, May 15). Court says law school may consider race in admissions. *New York Times,* p. A16.

Steinhorn, L., and Diggs-Brown, B. (1999). By the color of our skin: The illusion of integration and the reality of race. New York: Penguin.

Stiglitz, J. E. (1998). *Towards a new paradigm for development: Strategies, policies, and processes.* Paper presented at the Prebisch Lecture, UNCTAD, October 19, Geneva, Switzerland.

Sullivan, J., Esmail, A., and Soh, R. (2002). Interaction patterns between black and white college students: For better or worse? In R. Moore (Ed.), *The quality and quantity of contact: African Americans and whites on college campuses* (pp. 204–224). Lanham, MD: University Press of America.

Sutton, E. (1998). The role of the office of minority affairs in fostering cultural diversity. *College Student Affairs, 18,* 33–39.

Sztompka, P. (1979). *Sociological dilemmas: Toward a dialectic paradigm.* New York: Academic Press.

Tatum, B. (2000). The ABC approach to creating climates of engagement on diverse campuses. *Liberal Education, 86,* 22–29.

Taylor, E. (1995). Talking race in concrete: Leadership, diversity, and praxis. *Journal of Professional Studies, 3,* 61–68.

Tebbs, J., and Turner, S. (2005). College education for low-income students. *Change, 37,* 34–43.

Terenzini, P., Cabrera, A., and Colbeck, C. (2001). Racial and ethnic diversity in the classroom. *Journal of Higher Education, 72,* 509–531.

Thernstrom, A. (2000). Diversity yes, preferences no. *Academe, 5,* 30–33.

Thomas, D., and Ely, R. (1996). Making differences matter: A new paradigm for managing diversity. *Harvard Business Review, 74,* 79–90.

Thomas, I. (1994). The big chill. *Hispanic, 7,* 18–22.

Thorne-Beckerman, A. (1999). Postmodern organizational analysis: An alternative framework for school social workers. *Social Work in Education, 21,* 177–188.

Tichy, N., and Devanna, M. (1986). *The transformational leader.* New York: Wiley.

Tien, C. (1998). Challenges and opportunities for leaders of color. In L. Valverde and L. Castenell (Eds.), *The multicultural campus: Strategies for transforming higher education* (pp. 33–49). Walnut Creek, CA: AltaMira Press.

Tierney, W. (1989a). Advancing democracy: A critical interpretation of leadership. *Peabody Journal of Education, 89,* 157–175.

Tierney, W. (1989b). Cultural politics and the curriculum in postsecondary education. *Journal of Education, 171,* 72–88.

Tierney, W. (1992). Cultural leadership and the search for community. *Liberal Education, 78,* 16–21.

Tierney, W. (2000). Symbolism and presidential perceptions of leadership. In M. C. Brown II (Ed.), *Organization and governance in higher education* (5th ed.) (pp. 223–231). Boston: Pearson Custom Publishing.

Tierney, W. (2001). The autonomy of knowledge and the decline of the subject: Postmodernism and the reformulation of the university. *Higher Education, 41,* 353–372.

Trainer, J. F. (2004). Models and tools for strategic planning. *New Directions for Institutional Research, 123,* 129–138.

Trow, M. (1985). Comparative reflections on leadership in higher education. *European Journal of Education, 20,* 143–159.

Turner, C. (2003). Incorporation and marginalization in the academy. *Journal of Black Studies, 34,* 112–125.

Turner, C., and Myers, S. (2000). *Faculty of color in academe: Bittersweet success.* Boston: Allyn & Bacon.

Turner, R. (1996). The dangers of misappropriation: Misusing Martin Luther King Jr.'s legacy to prove the colorblind thesis. *Michigan Journal of Race and Law, 2,* 101–130.

Tyack, D., and Hansot, E. (1980). From social movement to professional management: An inquiry into the changing character of leadership in public education. *American Journal of Education, 88,* 291–319.

Umbach, P., and Kuh, G. (2003). *Student experiences and diversity in liberal arts colleges: Another claim for distinctiveness.* Paper presented at the 43rd Annual Forum for the Association for Institutional Research, May, Tampa, FL.

Vaughan, G. (1996). Paradox and promise: Leadership and the neglected minorities. *New Directions for Community Colleges, 94,* 5–12.

Vicere, A. (1995). The cycles of global leadership. *American Journal of Management Development, 1,* 11–17.

Wagner, A. (2005). Unsettling the academy: Working through the challenges of anti-racist pedagogy. *Race, Ethnicity and Education, 8,* 261–275.

Walker, A., and Quong, T. (1998). Valuing differences: Strategies for dealing with the tensions of educational leadership in a global society. *Peabody Journal of Education, 73,* 81–105.

Wallace, J. (2003). Ideology vs. reality: The myth of equal opportunity in a color-blind society. *Akron Law Review, 36,* 693–716.

Weinstein, D., and Weinstein, M. (1998). Is postmodern organization theory skeptical? *Journal of Management History, 4,* 350–362.

West, C. (1994). *Race matters.* Boston: Beacon Press.

Whetten, D., and Cameron, K. (1985). Administrative effectiveness in higher education. *Review of Higher Education, 9,* 35–49.

Wilcox, J., and Ebbs, S. (1992). *The leadership compass: Values and ethics in higher education.* Washington, DC: School of Education and Human Development, The George Washington University.

Williams, D. (2005). Seven recommendations for highly effective diversity officers. *Black Issues in Higher Education, 22,* 53.

Williams, T., Nakashima, C., Kich, G., and Reginald, D. (1996). Being different together in the university classroom: Multicultural identity as transgressive education. In P. Root (Ed.), *The multicultural experience: Racial borders as the new frontier* (pp. 359–379). Thousand Oaks, CA: Sage.

Williamson, C. (2000, July 24). Toigo foundation to establish its first endowment fund. *Pensions and Investments,* p. 43.

Winbush, R. (1999). Campus hate crimes: Fruit on the American tree of violence. *Black Collegian, 30,* 145–148.

Winston, M. (2001). The importance of leadership diversity: The relationship between diversity and organizational success in the academic environment. *College and Research Libraries, 62,* 517–526.

Wong, M., and Tierney, W. (2001). Reforming faculty work: Culture, structure and the dilemma of organizational change. *Teachers College Record, 103,* 1081–1101.

Wood, D. (2000, January 19). Minorities hope TV deals don't just lead to "tokenism." *Christian Science Monitor,* p. 3.

Yates, E. (2002). Auburn's long road to diversity. *Black Issues in Higher Education, 20,* 8–9.

Yukl, G. (1994). *Leadership in organizations* (3rd ed.). Englewood Cliffs, NJ: Prentice Hall.

Name Index

A

Agathangelou, A., 54
Aguirre, A., Jr., 25, 29, 41, 55–59, 62, 67, 71, 77, 87
Albino, J., 66
Alderfer, C., 41, 51
Alire, C., 86
Allen, W., 35, 71
Allison, M., 49
Altbach, P., 38
Amaral, A., 26
Amatea, E., 87
Andrews, H., 87
Araujo, L., 27
Arenson, K., 74
Argyris, C., 27, 28
Armour, S., 74
Arocena, R., 55
Arthur, J., 26, 36, 62
Astin, A., 25, 38
Astin, H., 25, 38
Astin, H., 18
Avolio, B. J., 36
Ayers, D., 29

B

Baker, O., 41, 49
Bakke, A., 4
Baldridge, J. V., 35, 65
Banks, J., 55
Bass, B., 60, 72
Battin, P., 40
Beane, J., 88

Beck, C., 29
Behar-Horenstein, L., 87
Benjamin, M., 60
Bensimon, E., 28, 31
Bergquist, W., 29
Bernard, E., 73
Berry, M., 76
Bess, J., 56, 60
Birnbaum, R., 28, 29, 31, 35, 82
Bjork, L., 60
Black, J., 30
Blau, P., 35
Blauner, R., 60
Bloland, H., 29
Bloom, A., 63
Blumberg, R., 82–83
Blumenthal, J., 56
Boggs, D. J., 7
Bok, D., 31, 53
Bollag, B., 73
Bond, M., 49
Bonilla-Silva, E., 76, 77
Borkowski, F., 39
Bowen, W., 31, 53
Bower, B., 59, 73
Brandt, R., 58
Bray, N. J., 33–34
Brayboy, B.M.J., 49, 56, 67
Bridges, B., 67
Bringle, R., 65
Brown, C., 59, 81
Brown, L., 34
Brown, M., 76, 77

Freed, J., 27
Fujita, E., 32
Fuller, B., 64, 65
Fullinder, R., 2

G

Gabor, A., 27
Gade, M., 32
Galis, L., 55
Gallos, J., 33
Garcia, M., 59, 61
Gephart, R., 27
Giles, C., 27
Goldman, P., 56, 60
Golembiewski, R., 26
Gratz, J., 6
Green, D., 59
Green, M., 82
Green, M., 82
Green-Merritt, E., 82
Gregory, M., 72
Grutter, B., 6
Gurin, P., 59, 63
Gutierrez, M., 73

H

Haberman, M., 33, 37
Hakuta, K., 54, 63
Hale, F., 44, 81
Hall, R., 48, 50
Hamacher, P., 6
Hansot, E., 48
Harding, N., 29
Hargreaves, A., 27
Haro, R., 58
Harris, A., 5
Hartley, D., 28
Hatcher, J., 65
Hays, C., 41
Heck, R., 31, 33
Heller, S., 78
Herbert, A., 84
Higgs, M., 58
Hill, B., 82
Holmes, M., 67
Hoojiberg, R., 26, 57

Hoover, J., 54
Hope, R., 80
Hopwood, C. J., 5
Hrabowski, F., 82–83
Hubbard, E., 60, 65, 82
Hu-Dehart, E., 72
Hudson, J., 62
Humphreys, D., 67
Hurtado, S., 35, 71
Hyter, M., 74

I

Ibarra, R., 42, 60
Ingle, G., 57

J

Jackson, J., 53, 85
Jacobs, K., 49
Jacobs, L., 38
Jaffee, D., 27
Jasis, R., 73
Johnson, J., 39
Johnsrud, L., 31, 33
Johnston, B., 87
Jones, J., 54, 63
Judkins, B., 56
Julius, D., 65
Jurik, N., 56
Justiz, M., 60

K

Karen, D., 35
Katsinas, S., 73
Keller, G., 65
Kelley, J., 64–65
Keough, T., 26, 36
Kerr, C., 32
Ketchen, D., 86
Keup, J., 18
Kezar, A., 28, 30, 31, 71, 87
Kich, G., 73
Killian, L., 76, 77
King, M. L., Jr., 76
Klugman, M., 27
Kohn, M., 55
Kotler, P., 64, 65

W

Wagner, A., 81
Waldman, D. A., 36
Walker, A., 18, 87
Wallace, J., 76
Walter, J., 60
Wang, L., 44
Ward, C., 62
Weiner, S., 61
Weinstein, D., 26
Weinstein, M., 26
West, C., 54
Whetten, D., 30
Wilcox, J., 19
Wildman, S., 5
Williams, D., 75
Williams, J., 67
Williams, T., 73

Williamson, C., 51
Wilson, R., 60
Winbush, R., 62
Winston, M., 39, 58, 60, 87
Witt, D., 54, 63
Wong, M., 32
Wood, D., 41

Y

Yammarino, F. J., 36
Yates, E., 75, 80
Yosso, T., 78
Young, P., 73
Yukl, G., 36

Z

Zalewski, M., 54

Subject Index

A

Academic Questions (National Association of Scholars, 64

Administrators, 16–17

Affirmative action, 2, 21

American Association of Community Colleges, Future Leaders Institute, 51

American Association of Medical Colleges, Faculty Development and Leadership, 52

American Association of State College and Universities, Millennium Leadership, 52

American Association of University Professors, 81

American Association of University Women, 55
Leadership and Training Institute, 52

American Council of Trustees and Alumni, 64

American Council on Education, 81
ACE Fellows Program, 52
Office of Women in Higher Education, National and Regional Leadership Forums, 52

American Indian Higher Education Consortium Leadership Fellows Program, 52

Association for Biblical Higher Education, Leadership Development for Biblical Higher Education, 52

Association of American Colleges and Universities, 55

Association of Colleges and Research Libraries, 52

Auburn University, 80

B

Bakke, University of California v., 2, 4, 5, 7, 8, 23, 71

Bollinger, Gratz v., 1, 6, 8, 12, 71

Bollinger, Grutter v., 1, 6, 8, 12, 47, 59, 71

Bush administration, 77

Business organizations, 49

C

California Supreme Court, 5

Campus diversity, competing perceptions of, 17–18

Center for Equal Opportunity, 64

Center for Individual Rights, 59

Civil Rights Act, 6

Coca-Cola, 49

Colorado State University, Pueblo (CSU-Pueblo), 78–80

Committee on Institutional Cooperation, CIC Academic Leadership Program, 52

Co-optation, 56

Co-optation, *versus* transformational strategies, 57–59

Council for Graduate Schools, Preparing Future Faculty Program, 52

CSU-Pueblo. *See* Colorado State University, Pueblo

Cultural proficiency, 86–87

About the Authors

Adalberto Aguirre Jr. is Chair and Professor in the Department of Sociology, University of California-Riverside. He has published articles and books in the areas of affirmative action, higher education equity, and race/class inequality. He is the author of the following ERIC monographs: (with R. Martinez) Chicano Faculty in Higher Education: Issues and Dilemmas for the 21st Century (1993); Women and Minority Faculty in the Academic Workplace: Recruitment, Retention, and Academic Culture (2000).

Rubén O. Martinez is a sociologist and professor of public administration at the University of Texas at San Antonio, where he also directs the Center for Policy Studies. He is a former senior academic administrator with applied interests in diversity and higher education. His research areas include diversity leadership, leadership and organizational change, education and ethnic minorities, youth development, and environmental justice. He is co-author of the ASHE-ERIC Higher Education Report, Chicanos in Higher Education: Issues and Dilemmas for the 21st Century (1993).

About the ASHE Higher Education Report Series

Since 1983, the ASHE (formerly ASHE-ERIC) Higher Education Report Series has been providing researchers, scholars, and practitioners with timely and substantive information on the critical issues facing higher education. Each monograph presents a definitive analysis of a higher education problem or issue, based on a thorough synthesis of significant literature and institutional experiences. Topics range from planning to diversity and multiculturalism, to performance indicators, to curricular innovations. The mission of the Series is to link the best of higher education research and practice to inform decision making and policy. The reports connect conventional wisdom with research and are designed to help busy individuals keep up with the higher education literature. Authors are scholars and practitioners in the academic community. Each report includes an executive summary, review of the pertinent literature, descriptions of effective educational practices, and a summary of key issues to keep in mind to improve educational policies and practice.

The Series is one of the most peer reviewed in higher education. A National Advisory Board made up of ASHE members reviews proposals. A National Review Board of ASHE scholars and practitioners reviews completed manuscripts. Six monographs are published each year and they are approximately 120 pages in length. The reports are widely disseminated through Jossey-Bass and John Wiley & Sons, and they are available online to subscribing institutions through Wiley InterScience (http://www.interscience.wiley.com).

Call for Proposals

The ASHE Higher Education Report Series is actively looking for proposals. We encourage you to contact one of the editors, Dr. Kelly Ward (kaward@wsu.edu) or Dr. Lisa Wolf-Wendel (lwolf@ku.edu), with your ideas.

Recent Titles

Back Issue/Subscription Order Form

Copy or detach and send to:
Jossey-Bass, A Wiley Imprint, 989 Market Street, San Francisco CA 94103-1741

Call or fax toll-free: Phone 888-378-2537 6:30AM – 3PM PST; Fax 888-481-2665

Back Issues: Please send me the following issues at $26 each
(Important: please include series abbreviation and issue number.
For example ASHE 28:1)

_____

_____

_____

$ _____ Total for single issues

$ _____ SHIPPING CHARGES: SURFACE   Domestic Canadian
                                    First Item $5.00 $6.00
                                    Each Add'l Item $3.00 $1.50
            For next-day and second-day delivery rates, call the number listed above.

Subscriptions Please ❑ start ❑ renew my subscription to *ASHE Higher Education Report* for the year 2_____ at the following rate:

U.S.	❑ Individual $165	❑ Institutional $199
Canada	❑ Individual $165	❑ Institutional $235
All Others	❑ Individual $201	❑ Institutional $310

❑ Online subscriptions available too!

**For more information about online subscriptions, visit
www.interscience.wiley.com**

$ _____ Total single issues and subscriptions (Add appropriate sales tax for your state for single issue orders. No sales tax for U.S. subscriptions. Canadian residents, add GST for subscriptions and single issues.)

❑Payment enclosed (U.S. check or money order only)
❑VISA ❑ MC ❑ AmEx ❑ #_____ Exp. Date _____

Signature _____ Day Phone _____
❑ Bill Me (U.S. institutional orders only. Purchase order required.)

Purchase order # _____
                 Federal Tax ID13559302   GST 89102 8052

Name _____

Address _____

_____

Phone _____ E-mail _____

For more information about Jossey-Bass, visit our Web site at www.josseybass.com

ASHE-ERIC HIGHER EDUCATION REPORT IS NOW AVAILABLE ONLINE AT WILEY INTERSCIENCE

What is Wiley InterScience?

Wiley InterScience is the dynamic online content service from John Wiley & Sons delivering the full text of over 300 leading scientific, technical, medical, and professional journals, plus major reference works, the acclaimed Current Protocols laboratory manuals, and even the full text of select Wiley print books online.

What are some special features of Wiley InterScience?

Wiley Interscience Alerts is a service that delivers table of contents via e-mail for any journal available on Wiley InterScience as soon as a new issue is published online.
Early View is Wiley's exclusive service presenting individual articles online as soon as they are ready, even before the release of the compiled print issue. These articles are complete, peer-reviewed, and citable.
CrossRef is the innovative multi-publisher reference linking system enabling readers to move seamlessly from a reference in a journal article to the cited publication, typically located on a different server and published by a different publisher.

How can I access Wiley InterScience?

Visit http://www.interscience.wiley.com.

Guest Users can browse Wiley InterScience for unrestricted access to journal Tables of Contents and Article Abstracts, or use the powerful search engine.
Registered Users are provided with a *Personal Home Page* to store and manage customized alerts, searches, and links to favorite journals and articles. Additionally, Registered Users can view free Online Sample Issues and preview selected material from major reference works.
Licensed Customers are entitled to access full-text journal articles in PDF, with select journals also offering full-text HTML.

How do I become an Authorized User?

Authorized Users are individuals authorized by a paying Customer to have access to the journals in Wiley InterScience. For example, a University that subscribes to Wiley journals is considered to be the Customer. Faculty, staff and students authorized by the University to have access to those journals in Wiley InterScience are Authorized Users. Users should contact their Library for information on which Wiley journals they have access to in Wiley InterScience.